# AS-Level
# Psychology

AS Psychology is seriously tricky — no question about that.
To do well, you're going to need to revise properly and practise hard.

This book has thorough notes on everything you need to know for the
OCR specification, plus plenty of detailed psychological studies.

There are also warm-up and exam-style practice questions for every topic,
with a separate section of advice on how to do well in the exams.

And of course, we've done our best to make the whole thing vaguely entertaining for you.

# Complete Revision and Practice
## Exam Board: OCR

Published by CGP

Editors:
Katherine Craig, Rachael Rogers, Camilla Simson.

Contributors:
Richard Carciofo, Dr Karen Goodall, Christine Johnson, Tracey Jones, Denise Say, Stuart Wilson.

ISBN 978 1 84762 994 4

With thanks to Ceara Hayden for the proofreading.

Groovy website: www.cgpbooks.co.uk

Jolly bits of clipart from CorelDRAW®
Printed by Elanders, Newcastle upon Tyne.

Based on the classic CGP style created by Richard Parsons.

# Contents

*We deliberately haven't put any answers in this book, because they'd just be saying what's already in the book. So instead, here's how to write answers and do well.*

# What is Psychology?

*These two pages give you a very quick intro to psychology. Don't spend ages learning this cos it's really just an overview of stuff you'll cover in detail later on.*

## Psychology is a Science with **Lots of Theories** and **Few Facts**

Psychology is "**the scientific study of experience and behaviour**."
This basically means that psychologists look at what people and animals do, why they do it, and how they feel.

A lot of psychology sounds like **common sense**, but it's a science, so everything's got to be investigated.
You've got to come up with a **theory** about something and then **scientifically test** it.

It's difficult to prove things in psychology, so there are loads of disagreements and a lot of theories that sound rubbish.
But you can't just say they're rubbish in your exam — that'd be too easy. No, you've got to use other theories and experiments to support your answer.

The different schools of thought are called **approaches**. Each approach has its own explanation for why we do what we do. You'll be looking at the **cognitive**, **physiological**, **developmental**, **social**, and **psychodynamic** approaches. Fortunately for you, they're split up into handy little sections.

## The **Cognitive Approach** Focuses on **Internal Processes**

The brain is a complex information processor.

1) Cognitive psychologists focus on **internal processes** to understand behaviour, such as how we perceive or remember things.

2) They compare the human mind to a **computer** system, so they use **computer models** to try to understand human cognition (thinking).

3) Using concepts from information processing, cognitive psychologists describe the brain as a **processor** — it receives **input**, **processes** it, and produces an **output**. Obviously it's ridiculously more complicated, but the general idea is the same.

4) Cognitive psychology studies are often laboratory-based and **artificial**, so they can lack **validity** in the **real world**. This is known as '**ecological validity**' (see page 26).

## **Developmental** Psychology is About How Humans **Develop**... Obviously...

Developmental psychology is a bit of a jumble of ideas from different approaches...

Developmental psychologists look at how people **develop** and **change** over their lifetime.
They place emphasis on the importance of **early experiences** in shaping the rest of a person's life.

> **Freud** (1909) believed that children go through stages of **psychosexual development**.
> There are five stages of **psychosexual development** — the oral, anal, phallic, latency and genital stages.
> If a child has a serious problem or excessive pleasure in any of these stages, they can become **fixated** with that stage. The **fixations** can continue into adult life and affect their behaviour.

In the second half of the 20th century psychologists started to look at how children are **qualitatively different** to adults in their understanding, abilities and feelings.

> Researchers like **Piaget** and **Samuel and Bryant** looked at children's **cognitive** development. They studied the way children approach problems depending on their age and the stage of development they've reached.
>
> They found that the brain appears to have a **timetable** of **what** we can do and **when** we can do it — e.g. children don't start speaking or progress with potty training until they reach a certain stage of development.

Alan won't be able to start growing until the nurse loosens her grip.

# What is Psychology?

## The *Physiological Approach* Explains Behaviour as a Product of *Nature*

There are three **key assumptions** in this approach:

 1 **Human behaviour** can be explained by looking at internal, biological stuff, like hormones and the nervous system.

 2 Experimental research that uses **animals** can tell us about **human behaviour** because we have similar biological make-ups.

 3 **Unwanted behaviour** can sometimes be changed for the better using **biological treatments** — e.g. medication for mental illness.

So, as far as this approach is concerned, it's what's inside that counts...

1) Researchers look at **genetics**, the **brain**, **hormones** and the **nervous system** to explain behaviour.
2) It's very scientific — research is mostly carried out in **laboratory experiments**.
3) Common research techniques include **brain scans** and **correlational studies**.

## *Individual Differences* is About *Differences* Between... erm... *Individuals*

This is another section that's made up of bits from loads of approaches. The main thing that researchers want to find out is **how** and **why** we're all **different** from each other. You might think it's pretty obvious that we're all different, but psychologists have got to find something to fill the day.

We all have different interests.

1) Other areas of psychology tend to assume that people are broadly the same — e.g. developmental psychologists assume that we all go through the same basic stages of development.
2) A big area of research is **abnormality**. Deviation from the norm is okay to a point, but societies have difficulties dealing with people who are considered to be very abnormal.
3) Because of this, an important issue to bear in mind is how **normality** is **defined**, and whether anyone has the right to decide that someone else is **abnormal**.

## *Social Psychologists* Look at How We *Interact* with Each Other

Last one, hurrah.

1) This approach is all about how we **influence** each other.
2) Major areas of research include **conformity** and **obedience**.
3) Society needs people to conform and be obedient in order to function properly — e.g. if drivers didn't abide by the rules of the road there would be chaos.
4) This can be a problem though, because people might be more likely to do something they think is wrong if they feel pressured by others.

Probably the most famous experiment in social psychology is **Milgram's Behavioural Study of Obedience** (1963). In the experiment he tested people's obedience by asking participants to give someone electric shocks. Most of his participants carried on giving the shocks, even when they thought they were causing harm. He concluded that most people will follow orders even if it means doing something they don't think is right. Pretty scary stuff. You can find this study on page 54.

## It's psychology, Jim, but not as we know it...

*There are so many different types of theory that call themselves 'psychology'. Some of them are a bit more like biology, some are more like computing, and some... are Freud's theories. The interesting thing about his weird ideas is that it's hard to prove them wrong. So they're still around and that means you've got to learn them.*

# The Scientific Process

*'How Science Works' is all about the scientific process — how we develop and test scientific ideas. It's what scientists do all day, every day. Well, except at coffee time. Never come between scientists and their coffee.*

## Science *Answers Real-life* Questions

Science tries to explain **how** and **why** things happen — it **answers questions**. It's all about seeking and gaining **knowledge** about the world around us. Scientists do this by **asking** questions and **suggesting** answers and then **testing** them, to see if they're correct — this is the **scientific process**.

The evidence supported Quentin's Theory of Flammable Burps.

1) **Ask** a question — make an **observation** and ask **why or how** it happens.

2) **Suggest** an answer, or part of an answer, by forming a **theory** (a possible explanation of the observations).

3) Make a **prediction** or **hypothesis** — a **specific testable statement**, based on the theory, about what will happen in a test situation.

4) Carry out a **test** — to provide **evidence** that will support the prediction (or help to disprove it).

Suggesting explanations is all very well and good, but if there's **no way to test** them then it just ain't science. A theory is **only scientific** if it can be tested.

## Science *is All About* Testing Theories

It starts off with one experiment backing up a prediction and theory. It ends up with all the scientists in the world **agreeing** with it and you **learning** it. Stirring stuff. This is how the magical process takes place:

1) The results are **published** — scientists need to let others know about their work, so they try to get their results published in **scientific journals**. These are just like normal magazines, only they contain **scientific reports** (called papers) instead of celebrity gossip. All work must undergo **peer review** before it's published.

- **Peer review** is a process used to **ensure the integrity** of published scientific work. Before publication, scientific work is sent to **experts** in that field (**peers**) so they can assess the **quality** of the work.

- This process helps to keep scientists **honest** — e.g. you can't '**sex-up**' your conclusions if the data doesn't support it, because it **won't pass** peer review.

- Peer review helps to **validate conclusions** — it means published theories, data and conclusions are more trustworthy. But it **can't guarantee** that the conclusions are 100% right. More **rounds** of predicting and testing are needed before they can be taken as '**fact**'.

- Sometimes **mistakes** are made and bad science is published. Peer review **isn't perfect** but it's probably the best way for scientists to **self-regulate** their work and to ensure **reliable** scientific work is **published**.

2) Other scientists read the published theories and results, and try to **repeat them** — this involves repeating the **exact experiments**, and using the theory to make **new predictions** that are tested by **new experiments**.

3) If all the experiments in all the world provide evidence to back it up, the theory is thought of as scientific 'fact' (**for now**).

4) If **new evidence** comes to light that **conflicts** with the current evidence the theory is questioned all over again. More rounds of **testing** will be carried out to see which evidence, and so which theory, **prevails**.

## If the **Evidence** *Supports a Theory, It's* **Accepted** *— For Now*

Our currently accepted theories have survived this '**trial by evidence**'. They've been tested **over and over and over** and each time the results have backed them up. **BUT**, and this is a big but (teehee), they never become totally undisputable fact. Scientific **breakthroughs or advances** could provide new ways to question and test a theory, which could lead to **changes and challenges** to it. Then the testing starts all over again...

And this, my friend, is the **tentative nature of scientific knowledge** — it's always **changing** and **evolving**.

# The Role of Science

*Science is all about the search for truth and knowledge.  But why bother?  We want to know as much as possible so we can use it to try to improve our lives (and because we're nosy).*

## Science Helps Us Make **Better Decisions**

Lots of scientific work eventually leads to **important discoveries** that could **benefit humankind**.  Oh yes.
These results are **used by society** (that's you, me and everyone else) to **make decisions** about the way we live.
All sections of society use scientific evidence to make decisions:

1) **Politicians** use science to devise policy.  E.g. **cognitive behavioural therapy** is available on the NHS because there's evidence to show it can help people with **depression**.

2) **Private organisations** use science to determine what to make or develop — e.g. evidence has shown that the number of people being diagnosed with **depression** is increasing, so drugs companies might put **more money** into this area of research.

3) **Individuals** also use science to make decisions about their **own lives** — e.g. evidence suggests that we should exercise and eat healthily, but it's up to individuals to **decide** whether they take that advice or not.

## Other **Factors** Can **Influence** Decision Making

Other factors can influence decisions about science or the way science is used:

**Economic factors**

- Society has to consider the **cost** of implementing changes based on scientific conclusions — e.g. the **NHS** can't afford the most expensive drugs without **sacrificing** something else.
- Scientific research is **expensive** so companies won't always develop new ideas — e.g. developing new drugs is costly, so pharmaceutical companies often only invest in drugs that are likely to make **money**.

**Social factors**

- **Decisions affect people's lives.**  How psychologists decide what's **normal** and what's **abnormal** affects how people are treated — e.g. homosexuality was defined as an **abnormal behaviour** until 1987.

**Environmental factors**

- Scientists believe **unexplored regions**, like parts of rainforests, might contain **untapped drug** resources. But some people think we shouldn't **exploit** these regions because any interesting finds might lead to **deforestation**, **reduced biodiversity** and **more $CO_2$** in the atmosphere.

## Science Has **Responsibilities**

Yes, you've guessed it — **ethics**.  Science has to be **responsible** in many ways.  Scientists aren't allowed to test something just because they can.  They have to think about the **ethical considerations** surrounding the experiment design and how the results could affect society.

1) **Design** — e.g. experiments involving **animals** are tightly controlled and monitored.  **Studies** are checked to ensure they aren't placing individuals in **unnecessary danger**.  If a study shows a drug has a highly **beneficial effect**, it's stopped and those in the **placebo** (negative) group are given the drug too.

2) **Results** — e.g. scientists' understanding of some **genetic disorders** could lead to tests to detect members of the population that carry the genes for them.  But would people want to know?

Society does have a say in what experiments take place.  **Controversial experiments** involving ethical issues have to be approved by scientific and **ethics councils** before they are allowed to be carried out.

## So there you have it — how science works...

*Hopefully these pages have given you a nice intro to how science works — what scientists do to provide you with 'facts'. You need to understand this, as you're expected to use it to evaluate evidence for yourselves — in the exam and in life.*

# Research Methods

*When a psychologist comes up with a theory they don't just sit there thinking "well isn't that a good idea..." — they test it out. This section is all about how they go about doing that. Are you sitting comfortably... then lets get stuck in.*

## Laboratory Experiments are Controlled and Scientific

1) An **experiment** is a way of conducting research in a **controlled** way.

2) The aim is to **control** all relevant variables except for **one key variable**, which is altered to see what the effect is. The variable that you alter is called the **independent variable** (see page 9).

3) Laboratory experiments are conducted in an **artificial setting**, e.g. Milgram's study (see page 54).

**Advantages**

**Control** — the effects of confounding variables (those that have an effect in addition to the variable of interest — see page 9) are minimised.

**Replication** — strict controls mean you can run the study again to check the findings.

**Causal relationships** — ideally it's possible to establish whether one variable actually causes change in another.

**Disadvantages**

**Artificial** — experiments might not measure real-life behaviour (i.e. they may lack ecological validity).

**Demand characteristics** — participants may respond according to what they think is being investigated, which can bias the results.

**Ethics** — deception is often used, making informed consent difficult.

## Field Experiments are Conducted Outside the Laboratory

In **field experiments** behaviour is measured in a **natural environment** like a school, the street or on a train. A **key variable** is still altered so that its effect can be measured.

**Advantages**

**Causal relationships** — you can still establish causal relationships by manipulating the key variable and measuring its effect, although it's very difficult to do in a field experiment.

**Ecological validity** — field experiments are less artificial than those done in a laboratory, so they relate to real life better.

**Demand characteristics** (participants trying to guess what the researcher expects from them and performing differently because of it) — these can be avoided if participants don't know they're in a study.

**Disadvantages**

**Less control** — confounding variables may be more likely in a natural environment.

**Ethics** — participants who didn't agree to take part might experience distress and often can't be debriefed. Observation must respect privacy.

## Natural Experiments Measure but Don't Control Variables

A **natural experiment** is a study that measures variables that **aren't** directly manipulated by the experimenter. For example, comparing behaviour in a single-sex school and a mixed school.

**Advantages**

**Ethical** — it's possible to study variables that it would be unethical to manipulate, e.g. you can compare a community that has TV with a community that doesn't to see which is more aggressive.

**Disadvantages**

**Participant allocation** — you can't randomly allocate participants to each condition, and so confounding variables (e.g. what area the participants live in) may affect results. Let's face it — you've got no control over the variables so it's ridiculously hard to say what's caused by what.

**Rare events** — some groups of interest are hard to find, e.g. a community that doesn't have TV.

**Ethics** — deception is often used, making informed consent difficult. Also, confidentiality may be compromised if the community is identifiable.

## Naturalistic Observation — Observing but NOT Interfering

**Naturalistic observation** involves observing subjects in their natural environment. Researchers take great care not to interfere in any way with the subjects they're studying.

**Advantages**

**Ecological validity** — behaviour is natural and there are no demand characteristics, as the participant is unaware of being observed.

**Theory development** — can be a useful way of developing ideas about behaviour that could be tested in more controlled conditions later.

**Disadvantages**

**Extraneous variables** — can't control variables that may affect behaviour.

**Observer bias** — observers' expectations may affect what they focus on and record. This means the reliability of the results may be a problem — another observer may have come up with very different results.

**Ethics** — you should only conduct observations where people might expect to be observed by strangers. This limits the situations where you can do a naturalistic observation. Debriefing is difficult. Observation must respect privacy. Getting informed consent can be tricky.

# Research Methods

## Correlational Research Looks for Relationships Between Variables

**Correlation** means that two variables rise and fall together, or that one rises as the other falls — but **not** always that one variable **causes** a change in the other, e.g. as age increases so might intelligence, but ageing doesn't **cause** intelligence.

**Advantages**
**Causal relationships** — these can be ruled out if no correlation exists.
**Ethics** — can study variables that would be unethical to manipulate, e.g. is there a relationship between the number of cigarettes smoked and incidences of ill health?

**Disadvantages**
**Causal relationships** — these cannot be assumed from a correlation, which may be caused by a third, unknown variable.
**Ethics** — misinterpretation can be an issue. Sometimes the media (and researchers) infer causality from a correlation.

## Questionnaires — Written, Face-to-Face, on the Phone, or via the Internet

**Advantages** **Practical** — can collect a large amount of information quickly and relatively cheaply.

**Disadvantages**
**Bad questions** — leading questions (questions that suggest a desired answer) or unclear questions can be a problem.
**Biased samples** — some people are more likely to respond to a questionnaire, which might make a sample unrepresentative.
**Self report** — people sometimes want to present themselves in a good light (social desirability bias — see page 15). What they say and what they actually think could be different, making any results unreliable.
**Ethics** — confidentiality can be a problem, especially around sensitive issues.

## Interviews — More Like a Conversation than a Face-to-Face Questionnaire

**Structured interviews** follow a fixed set of questions that are the same for all participants.
**Unstructured interviews** may have a set of discussion topics, but are less constrained about how the conversation goes.

**Advantages**
**Rich data** — can get detailed information, as there are fewer constraints than with a questionnaire. Unstructured interviews provide richer information than structured interviews.
**Pilot study** — interviews are a useful way to get information before a study.

**Disadvantages**
**Self report** — can be unreliable and affected by social desirability bias (see questionnaires).
**Impractical** — conducting interviews can be time-consuming and requires skilled researchers.
**Ethics** — confidentiality can be a problem, especially around sensitive issues.

## Case Studies are Intensive Descriptions of a Single Individual or Case

**Case studies** allow researchers to analyse unusual cases in a lot of detail, e.g. Freud's study of **Little Hans** (page 37).

**Advantages**
**Rich data** — researchers have the opportunity to study rare phenomena in a lot of detail.
**Unique cases** — can challenge existing ideas and theories, and suggest ideas for future research.

**Disadvantages**
**Causal relationships** — the researcher has very little control over variables.
**Generalisation** — only using a single case makes generalising the results extremely difficult.
**Ethics** — informed consent can be difficult to obtain if the subject has a rare disorder.

## Practice Questions

Q1 Describe a disadvantage of studies where correlational analysis is used.
Q2 What are the main advantages of laboratory experiments?
Q3 Why might you get an unrepresentative sample when carrying out questionnaire-based research?

**Exam Questions**

Q1 Describe what a field experiment is and outline its main advantages and disadvantages. [4 marks]

Q2 Describe the two types of interview a researcher might conduct.
Outline the main differences between them. [4 marks]

# Aims and Hypotheses

*When research is conducted, the idea is to carry out an **objective test** of something, i.e. to obtain a scientific measurement of how people behave — not just someone's opinion. Well that's what I reckon anyway...*

## Research Aims are Important

An **aim** is a statement of a study's purpose — for example Loftus and Palmer's aim might have been: 'To investigate the effects that leading questions have on the ability to accurately recall events'.

Research should state its aim **beforehand** so that it's **clear** what the study intends to investigate.

*See page 28 for the detail of Loftus and Palmer's (1974) study.*

## Hypotheses are Theories Tested by Research

Although the **aim** states the **purpose** of a study, it isn't usually **precise** enough to **test**. What is needed are clear statements of what's actually being tested — the **hypotheses**.

1) **RESEARCH HYPOTHESIS**

   The **research hypothesis** is proposed at the beginning of a piece of research and is often generated from a theory. For example — Baron-Cohen et al's (1997) research hypothesis was that adults with Asperger syndrome have an impaired theory of mind. (See page 33 for the details of this study.)

2) **NULL HYPOTHESIS**

   The **null hypothesis** is what you're going to **assume is true** during the study. Any data you collect will either back this assumption up, or it won't. If the data **doesn't support** your null hypothesis, you **reject** it and go with your **alternative hypothesis** instead.

   Very often, the null hypothesis is a prediction that there will be **no relationship** between key variables in a study — and any correlation is due to **chance**. (An example might be that there is no difference in exam grades between students who use a revision guide and students who don't.)

   (Note: It's quite usual to have something you **don't actually believe** as your null hypothesis. You assume it **is** true for the duration of the study, then if your results lead you to reject this null hypothesis, you've **proved** it **wasn't true** after all.)

3) **EXPERIMENTAL HYPOTHESIS (or ALTERNATIVE HYPOTHESIS)**

   If the data forces you to **reject** your null hypothesis, then you accept your **experimental (alternative) hypothesis** instead.

   So if your null hypothesis was that two variables **aren't** linked, then your alternative hypothesis would be that they **are** linked. Or you can be more specific, and be a bit more precise about **how** they are linked, using **directional** hypotheses (see below).

4) **DIRECTIONAL HYPOTHESIS**

   A hypothesis might predict a difference between the exam results obtained by two groups of students — a group that uses a revision guide and another group that doesn't.

   If the hypothesis states which group will do better, it is making a **directional prediction**.

   For example, you might say that students who use a revision guide will get **higher** exam grades than students who don't — this is a directional hypothesis.

   Directional hypotheses are often used when **previous research findings** suggest which way the results will go.

5) **NON-DIRECTIONAL HYPOTHESIS**

   A **non-directional hypothesis** would predict a difference, but wouldn't say which group would do better.

   For example, you might just say that there will be a **difference** in exam grades between students who use a revision guide and students who don't — this is a **non-directional** hypothesis, since you're not saying which group will do better.

   Non-directional hypotheses can be used when there is **little previous research** in the area under investigation, or when previous research findings are **mixed** and **inconclusive**.

# Aims and Hypotheses

## Some Variables are Manipulated by the Researcher — Others Aren't

A **variable** is a quantity whose **value** can **change** — for example, the time taken to do a task, anxiety levels, or exam results. There are various different kinds of variable.

### The Independent Variable is Directly Manipulated

1) An **independent variable** (**IV**) is a variable **directly manipulated** by the researcher.

2) In the example on the previous page about students, exams and revision guides, there are two variables. One is 'whether or not a revision guide is used' (so this variable has only two possible values: yes or no). The other is the 'exam grade' (and this could have lots of possible values: e.g. A, B, C, D, E, N, U).

3) In this case, the **independent variable** is 'whether or not a revision guide is used' — since this is **directly** under the control of the researcher.

### The Dependent Variable is Only Affected Indirectly

1) The **dependent variable** (**DV**) is the variable that you think is **affected** by changes in the independent variable. (So the DV is **dependent on** the **IV**.)

2) In the exam grades example, the dependent variable is the 'exam grade'. The exam grade is dependent on whether a revision guide was used (or at least, that's what's being **investigated**).

### Situation Variables Can't be Controlled but Might Still Affect What You're Measuring

1) Ideally in a study the *only* thing that would influence the **DV** (the thing you're measuring) would be the **IV** (the thing you're manipulating). Usually though, there are other things that will have an effect. This can be due to the **situation** or the **participants** taking part.

2) An **extraneous variable** is any variable (other than the **IV**) that **could** affect what you're trying to measure. If these things **are** actually **influencing** the DV then they're called **confounding variables**.

3) **Situation variables** might include the time of day students sit the exam (tiredness could be important), or whether they used different revision guides when studying (some guides might be better than others, and the study doesn't state that all students have to use the same one).

4) **Participant variables** are things specific to individuals that might also influence the results, such as age, gender, anxiety levels, intelligence or personality.

### Operationalisation is Showing How the Variables Will Be Measured

1) Variables must be **operationalised**. This means describing the **process** by which the variable is **measured**.

2) Some things are easy to operationalise (e.g. **height** might be operationalised as 'the distance in centimetres from the bottom of an object to the top'). Other things are difficult to operationalise (e.g. a mother's love for her newborn baby).

3) **Operationalisation** allows others to see exactly how you're going to define and measure your variables. It also has 18 letters, which is the same as soporiferousnesses, or yaaaaaaawwwwwwwwwwn.

## Practice Questions

Q1 What is the difference between a directional and non-directional hypothesis?
Q2 When would you reject the null hypothesis?
Q3 What is an independent variable?

**Exam Questions**

Q1 Bruno is interested in whether taking fish oil supplements every day for a month can improve memory performance. What would an appropriate experimental hypothesis be for his study? [2 marks]

Q2 Identify the dependent variable in Bruno's study. [1 mark]

## Aim to learn this page — I hypothesise you'll need it...

*Remember, you assume the null hypothesis is true unless your data suggests otherwise — if it does then you quickly switch allegiance to the alternative hypothesis instead. And remember, the IV is deliberately manipulated by the researcher. This might lead to an effect on the DV, but it's often a kind of indirect, knock-on effect. Yep, I agree — that's enough.*

# Research Design

*Once you've got a theory and your hypothesis sorted, this is how you'd actually go about testing it...*

## The Research Design Must Make the Hypothesis **Testable**

> **Research example** — does the presence of an audience help or hinder people doing the 'wiggly wire' task (moving a loop along a wire without touching it and setting off the buzzer)?
> Based on previous research, we expect people to do this better without anyone watching them.

1) The IV (the variable being manipulated) is the presence or absence of an audience.

2) The DV (the variable being measured) is 'how well' the participants do on the task — but it must be testable. You need a **precisely defined** (or **operationalised**) DV, which should be **quantitative** wherever possible. An operationalised DV for this experiment might be 'the time taken to move the loop from one end of the wire to the other without setting off the buzzer'.

## There are Three **Research Designs** that are Used Loads

1) An **independent groups design** means there are **different participants** in each group. Here, for example, one group does the task **with** an audience and another group does it **alone**. This avoids the problem that if all the participants did the test in both conditions, any improvement in performance might be due to them having two goes at the task (which would be a confounding variable).

| *Advantages* | *Disadvantages* |
|---|---|
| No **order effects** — no one gets better through practice (**learning effect**) or gets worse through being bored or tired (**fatigue effect**). | **Participant variables** — differences between the **people** in each group might affect the results (e.g. the 'without audience' group may just have people who are better at the task — so we can't safely compare groups). **Number of participants** — **twice as many** participants are needed to get the same amount of data, compared to having everyone do both conditions. |

2) A **repeated measures design** is where, e.g., all participants do the task both **with** an audience and then **without**. You can compare the performances in each condition, knowing the differences weren't due to participant variables.

| *Advantages* | *Disadvantages* |
|---|---|
| **Participant variables** — now the same people do the test in both conditions, so any differences between individuals shouldn't affect the results. **Number of participants** — **fewer** participants are needed to get the same amount of data. | **Order effects** — if all participants did the 'with audience' condition first, any improvements in the second condition could be due to **practice**, not the audience's absence. (But see **counterbalancing** on the next page.) |

3) A **matched pairs design** means there are different participants in each condition, but they're **matched** on important variables (like age, sex and personality). Some studies use **control groups**. These groups have not experienced any of the manipulations of the **IV** that an experimental group might have. This allows the researcher to make a direct comparison between them. In the example above the group that didn't have an audience would be the control group.

| *Advantages* | *Disadvantages* |
|---|---|
| No **order effects** — there are **different people** in each condition. **Participant variables** — important differences are minimised through **matching**. | **Number of participants** — need twice as many people compared to repeated measures. **Practicalities** — **time-consuming** and difficult to find participants who **match**. |

## It's Sometimes Good to Run a Small **Pilot Study** First

1) No piece of research is perfect. To help foresee any problems, a small-scale **pilot study** can be run first.

2) This should establish whether the **design** works, whether **participants** understand the wording in the **instructions**, or whether something important has been **missed out**.

3) Problems can be tackled before running the **main study**, which could save wasting a lot of **time** and **money**.

# Research Design

## Variables Can Be 'Controlled' so Their Unwanted Effects are Minimised

**Counterbalancing** (mixing up the order of the tasks) can solve **order effects** in **repeated measures** designs. Half the participants do the task **with** an audience **first** and **then without**. The others do the conditions **the other way round**. Any order effects would then be equal across conditions.

**Random allocation** (e.g. by drawing names out of a hat) means everyone has an **equal chance** of doing **either** condition. An **independent measures** study with, for example, more men in one group than the other could have a confounding variable. Any difference in performance may be due to **sex** rather than the real IV. Random allocation should ensure groups are **not biased** on key variables.

**Extraneous variables** can be controlled by:  (i)  keeping them **constant** for all participants (e.g. everyone does the task in the same place so distractions are similar),

(ii)  eliminating them altogether (e.g. everyone does the task somewhere with no noise distractions — shhhh...).

**Standardised instructions** should ensure the **experimenters** act in a similar way with all participants. Everything should be **as similar as possible** for all the participants, including each participant's **experience** in such studies.

## Researchers have to Consider Reliability and Validity

### Reliability

- If a test is consistent within itself, it has **internal reliability**. The **split-half technique** assesses this. A questionnaire is randomly split in two — if all participants score similarly on both halves, the questions measure the same thing.
- If the measure is stable over time or between people, then it has **external reliability**. This can be assessed by measuring **test-retest reliability** (does the same person always score similarly on the test?) or **inter-rater reliability** (do different assessors agree, i.e. do they both give the same score?).

### Validity

- If an experiment shows that the results were caused by the manipulation of the **variables**, rather than the effect of something else, then it has **internal validity**.
- If the findings can be **generalised** beyond the experimental setting (e.g. to different groups of people or different settings), then the experiment has **external validity**.

## Research Should be Designed with Ethical Issues in Mind

**Ethical guidelines** assist researchers who have **ethical dilemmas,** and should ensure that research is **acceptable** and participants are **protected**.

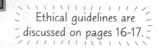
Ethical guidelines are discussed on pages 16-17.

## Practice Questions

Q1  Give one disadvantage of an independent groups design.

Q2  Give one design that overcomes the disadvantage you identified in Q1.

Q3  What are the main benefits of running a pilot study?

**Exam Questions**

Q1  a)  Why might a researcher choose to use a repeated measures design instead of an independent groups design? [2 marks]

b)  What could the researcher do to minimise any order effects that might influence the results? [2 marks]

## Inter-test validity, no... split-rater ethics, no... oh sod it.... zzzzzzzzz...

*There are a lot of details here, but they're all really important. If you're not really careful when you design a piece of research, the results you get might not be worth the paper you end up writing them down on. And that'd be no good. Spending a little bit of time thinking at the design stage will make it all worth it in the end — trust me.*

# Observations, Questionnaires and Interviews

*These pages will tell you everything you need to know about **naturalistic observation** — the collection of data by observing participants in their natural environments. Oh, and questionnaires. And interviews... Gosh, exciting times...*

## Researchers *can use* Participant *or* Non-Participant Observation

1) **Participant observation** is when the researcher **participates** in the activity under study in an **overt** way (their presence is obvious to the other participants).

   <u>Advantages</u> — The researcher develops a relationship with the group under study, so they can gain a greater understanding of the group's behaviour.

   <u>Disadvantages</u> — The researcher loses objectivity by becoming part of the group.
   — The participants may act differently if they know a researcher is amongst them.

2) **Non-participant observation** is when the researcher observes the activity without getting involved in it. This is a **covert** technique (their presence is unknown to the participants).

   <u>Advantages</u> — The researcher can remain objective throughout the study.

   <u>Disadvantages</u> — The researcher loses a sense of the group dynamics by staying separate from the group.

   Sometimes researchers undertake **structured observations**. This is where the behaviour categories that are going to be used are defined in **advance**.
   <u>Advantages</u> — It's easier to gather relevant data because you already know what you're looking for.
   <u>Disadvantages</u> — Interesting behaviours could go unrecorded because they haven't been pre-defined as important.

## Naturalistic Observation *Involves Making* Design Decisions

There are various ways of organising **structured observations** to make sure no behaviours are missed.

| | |
|---|---|
| Recording Data | If you want **qualitative data** you could just make **written notes**. But **video** or **audio recording** means that you have a more accurate permanent record. |
| Categorising Behaviour | You must **define** the behaviours you aim to observe. For example, if you were going to observe children in a school playground to see how many behave aggressively, you'd have to decide **what counts as aggression**. This involves giving an **operationalised definition** (i.e. some **specific, observable** behaviours). For example, you might say that *'aggression is any physical act made with the intention to harm another person — such as punching, kicking, etc.'* But you have to be careful not to **miss out** anything important otherwise your definition may not be valid, e.g. aggression can also be verbal. |
| Rating Behaviour | The behaviours that you're interested in may be things that are a matter of **degree**, so you might need to use a rating scale to classify behaviour. You could put each participant's behaviour into one of several **categories**, e.g. *not aggressive, mildly aggressive* or *very aggressive*. Or you could use a **coding system** where each participant is given a **number** (e.g. between 1 and 10) to represent how aggressive they are, where a **higher score** indicates **more aggression**. However, you still have to **define** what kinds of behaviour are included for each number on the scale (e.g. 5 = *pushing* and 10 = *kicking or punching more than once*). Behaviour rated in this way provides **quantitative data** (data in the form of **numbers**). |
| Sampling Behaviour | You have to decide **how often** and for **how long** you're going to observe the participants. **Event sampling** — this is when you only record particular events that you're interested in (e.g. aggression shown by the children) and ignore other behaviours. <u>Advantages</u> — Researchers know exactly what behaviours they're looking for. <u>Disadvantages</u> — Potentially interesting behaviours could be ignored. **Time-interval sampling** — if the behaviours occur over a long time period you might choose to observe for only set time intervals e.g. the first 10 minutes of every hour. The time intervals could be chosen randomly. <u>Advantages</u> — Very convenient for the researchers to carry out. <u>Disadvantages</u> — If interesting behaviours occur outside the time sample they won't be recorded. |
| Inter-Observer Reliability | Even after you've **defined** the behaviours you're interested in, you have to make sure that the observers are actually putting each participant in the **right category** or giving the **right rating**. This might involve **comparing** the data from two or more observers to make sure they're giving the **same** scores (i.e. that they are 'reliable'). |

# Observations, Questionnaires and Interviews

## Questionnaires Need to be Designed Carefully

There are various things you need to consider when designing a questionnaire for a survey.

1) **Type of data** — whether you want **qualitative data** and/or **quantitative data** will affect whether you ask **open** and/or **closed questions**.

   a) **Open questions** are questions such as *What kinds of music do you like?*
   The participant can reply in **any way**, and in as much detail as they want. This gives detailed, qualitative information, although it may be **hard to analyse**, as the participants could give very different answers.

   b) **Closed questions** limit the answers that can be given, e.g. *Which do you like: Pop, Rock or neither?*
   They give **quantitative** data that is relatively **easy to analyse** — e.g. you can say exactly **how many** people liked each type of music. However, less detail is obtained about each participant.

2) **Ambiguity** — you have to avoid questions and answer options which are **not** clearly **defined**,
   e.g. *Do you listen to music frequently?* What is meant here by 'frequently'? — Once a day, once a week?

3) **Double-barrelled questions** — best not to use these, since a person may wish to answer **differently** to each part.
   For example, *Do you agree that modern music is not as good as the music of the 1960s and that there should be more guitar-based music in the charts?*

4) **Leading questions** — these are questions that **lead** the participant towards a particular answer. E.g. *How old was the boy in the distance?* They might have seen an older person, but by saying '*boy*' you're leading them to describe the person as young. You're also leading them to think that the person was male, but they might not have been sure. (It's really important to avoid leading questions in **eyewitness testimony** — see page 28.)

5) **Complexity** — whenever possible **clear English** should be used, avoiding **jargon**.
   However, if specialist terms are included, they should be clearly defined.
   (So the question *Do you prefer music written in unusual time signatures?* probably isn't ideal for most people.)

## All of the Above Goes For Interviews As Well

But you also have to consider the following:

1) **How structured** the interview will be:
   Interviews can be very **informal** with **few set questions**, and new questions being asked **depending on** the participant's **previous answers**. This gives detailed qualitative data, which may be difficult to analyse. Alternatively, they may be more **structured**, with set questions and **closed answers**, giving **less detail** but being **easier to analyse**.

2) Using a **question checklist** — if the interview is structured, a checklist ensures that no questions are left out and questions aren't asked twice.

3) The behaviour or appearance of the **interviewer** — this could **influence** how the participants react.

## Practice Questions

Q1 How can behaviour be sampled in observational studies?

Q2 Give two ways of rating behaviour in observational studies.

Q3 Explain three of the issues involved in designing questionnaires and interviews.

**Exam Questions**

Q1 a) Outline what is meant by an 'open question'. [2 marks]
   b) For both open and closed questions, give one strength and one weakness of their use in a questionnaire. [6 marks]

Q2 What are the advantages of choosing a participant observation design instead of a non-participant observation design? [6 marks]

## Big Brother — naturalistic observation at its finest...?

*This is all about observing behaviour that's as natural as possible. What you don't want is for people to put on an act just because they're aware that they're being watched — that defeats the object of doing the study in the first place. Makes you wonder about Big Brother — can they keep an act up for all those weeks, or do we actually get to see some natural stuff?*

# Selecting and Using Participants

*These two pages are all about your participants — how to select them and how to keep them ~~under control~~ happy, so that they ~~won't do crazy things~~ will behave as naturally as possible. Do it wrong and it could really mess up your study...*

## Selecting a **Sample** of Participants Can Be Done in **Three Main Ways**

The part of a **population** that you're interested in studying (e.g. all the people in a particular city, or all people of a certain age or background) is called the **target group**. Usually you can't include everyone in the target group in a study, so you choose a certain **sample** of **participants**.

This sample should be **representative**, i.e. it should reflect the variety of characteristics that are found in the target group. A sample that is unrepresentative is **biased**. There are various methods of selecting a sample:

### Random Sampling

This is when **every** member of the target group has an **equal chance** of being selected for the sample. This could be done by giving everyone in the target group a number and then getting a computer to randomly pick numbers to select the participants. Sounds like being in a catalogue store. Order number 103 to the collection point...

*Advantages*: Random sampling is 'fair'. Everyone has an equal chance of being selected and the sample is **likely** to be representative.

*Disadvantages*: This method doesn't **guarantee** a representative sample — there's still a chance that some subgroups in the target group may not be selected (e.g. people from a minority cultural group).
Also, if the target group is large it may not be practical (or possible) to give everyone a number that might be picked. So in practice, completely random samples are rarely used.

### Opportunity Sampling

This is when the researcher samples whoever is **available and willing** to be studied. Since many researchers work in universities, they often use opportunity samples made up of students.

*Advantages*: This is a **quick** and **practical** way of getting a sample.

*Disadvantages*: The sample is **unlikely** to be **representative** of a target group or population as a whole. This means that we can't confidently **generalise** the findings of the research.
However, because it's **quick** and **easy**, opportunity sampling is **often used**.

### Self-Selected Sampling (Also Known as **Volunteer** Sampling)

This is when people actively **volunteer** to be in a study by responding to a request for participants advertised by the researcher, e.g. in a newspaper, or on a notice board.
The researcher may then select only those who are **suitable** for the study.
(This method was used by Milgram — see page 54.)

*Advantages*: If an advert is placed prominently (e.g. in a national newspaper) a **large number** of people may respond, giving more participants to study. This may allow more **in-depth analysis** and **more accurate** statistical results.

*Disadvantages*: Even though a large number of people may respond, these will only include people who actually saw the advertisement — no one else would have a chance of being selected.
Also, people who volunteer may be more **cooperative** than others. For these reasons the sample is **unlikely** to be **representative** of the target population.

No method can guarantee a representative sample, but you should have confidence that your sample is (quite) representative if you want to generalise your results to the entire target group.

# Selecting and Using Participants

## Participants Sometimes *Act Differently* When They're Being *Observed*

Human participants will usually be aware that they are being **studied**. This may mean they don't show their **true response**, and so their data may not be **valid** or **reliable**. Some of these effects are explained below...

 **THE HAWTHORNE EFFECT**: If people are **interested** in something and in the attention they are getting (e.g. from researchers), then they show a more **positive** response, try **harder** at tasks, and so on.

This means their results for tests are often **artificially high** (because they're trying harder than normal), which could make a researcher's conclusions **inaccurate**.

The opposite effect may occur if the participants are **uninterested** in the task.

 **DEMAND CHARACTERISTICS**: This is when participants form an idea about the **purpose** of a study. If they think they know what kind of response the researcher is **expecting** from them, they may show that response to '**please**' the researcher (or they may **deliberately** do the **opposite**).

Either way, the conclusions drawn from the study would be **inaccurate**.

 **SOCIAL DESIRABILITY BIAS**: People usually try to show themselves in the **best possible light**.

So in a survey, they may **not** be completely **truthful**, but give answers that are more **socially acceptable** instead (e.g. people may say they give more money to charity than they really do).

This would make the results **less accurate**.

## The *Researchers* Can *Affect* the Outcomes in *Undesirable Ways*

The **reliability** and **validity** of results may also be influenced by the researcher, since he or she has **expectations** about what will happen. This can produce the following effects:

 **RESEARCHER (or EXPERIMENTER) BIAS**: The researchers' **expectations** can influence how they **design** their study and how they **behave** towards the participants, which may then produce **demand characteristics**. Also, their expectations may influence **how** they take **measurements** and **analyse** their data, resulting in errors that can lead, for example, to accepting a hypothesis that was actually false.

 **INTERVIEWER EFFECTS**: The interviewer's **expectations** may lead them to ask only questions about what **they** are **interested** in, or to ask **leading questions**.

Or, they may **focus** on the aspects of the participant's answers which **fit** their **expectations**.

Also, the participant may react to the **behaviour** or **appearance** of an interviewer and then not answer truthfully.

## Practice Questions

Q1 Give a disadvantage of opportunity sampling.
Q2 Give an advantage of self-selected sampling.
Q3 What are demand characteristics?
Q4 How might a researcher's expectations affect a study?

**Exam Questions**

Q1 a) Outline one type of sampling technique that a researcher might use when recruiting people for a study. [2 marks]
 b) Give one strength and one weakness of this sampling strategy. [4 marks]

## Volunteers needed for study into pain and embarrassment... (and stupidity)

*In a study you could survey everyone in the world, but it might be expensive and time-consuming. This is why in most cases it's better to survey just a sample of participants. But you have to be careful how you choose them. There's no point in going to your local club and surveying all the crazy dancing people, cos I bet down at the old folk's home they'd disagree.*

# Ethical Issues in Psychological Research

*Ethics are standards about what's right and wrong, so an ethical issue is a dilemma about whether a study is acceptable and justified. Have a flick through this book and try to imagine yourself as a participant in some of the studies — ask yourself if you would've been happy taking part, how you'd have felt, and if it would've had long-term effects on you.*

## The British Psychological Society (BPS) Produces **Ethical Guidelines**

The **British Psychological Society** (BPS) has developed ethical guidelines to help psychologists resolve ethical issues in research and protect participants. They include advice on **deception**, **consent** and **psychological harm**.

### **Deception** Means Misleading or Withholding Information from Participants

Milgram (see page 54) deceived participants about his study's purpose and about the confederates who pretended to be real participants. Without deception the aim of this study could not be achieved. If deception has to be used, participants should be told of the true nature of the research as soon as possible, during the debriefing.

> **BPS Guidelines for Deception**
>
> Deception should be avoided wherever possible and only be used when it's scientifically justified — when the study would be meaningless otherwise.
>
> Deception shouldn't be used if it's likely that the participant will be unhappy when they discover the study's true nature.

### **Informed Consent** Should be Given Where Possible

Giving consent means **agreeing** to participate in a study. When a participant is told the research aim and procedure and then agrees to it, this is **informed consent**. They are fully informed before their decision to participate. If deception is used, participants **can't** give informed consent until they've been debriefed.

Milgram's participants **did not** give informed consent when they agreed to take part. They were deceived about aspects of the study and didn't have enough information for an informed decision.

> **BPS Guidelines for Informed Consent**
>
> Participants should be given all the information they need to decide whether to participate in research and shouldn't be coerced or pressured.
>
> Some people may not be able to give real informed consent — for example children. In these cases informed consent should be obtained from parents or guardians.

### **Psychological Harm** Means Any **Negative Emotion** (e.g. Stress, Distress, Embarrassment)

Milgram's participants may have experienced **stress** and were probably **embarrassed** about being 'tricked'.

> **BPS Guidelines for Psychological Harm**
>
> Researchers have a responsibility to protect participants from physical and psychological harm during the study. Any risk of harm should be no greater than what the participant might experience in their normal life.

## **Researchers** Have to Deal with **Ethical Issues in Their Studies**

**Deception**

Sometimes it's difficult to conduct meaningful research without a bit of **deception**. If participants know exactly what's being studied then their behaviour might change, and the data you get would be useless. Psychologists don't usually tell participants every last detail, but they do try to minimise deception. That way participants aren't likely to be upset when they find out the true nature of the study.
**Milgram's** experiment (page 54) is an example of a study that would probably not be considered ethical today. He deceived participants about the true purpose of the study and many of them showed signs of **stress** when taking part.

**Consent**

Gaining consent is central to conducting research ethically. But telling participants they're being observed could **change** the way they **behave**.
**Milgram's** participants couldn't give informed consent until after they were debriefed. If they'd known about the nature of the study, it wouldn't have worked.

# Ethical Issues in Psychological Research

## Confidentiality and Animal Rights are Also Ethical Issues

**Confidentiality means keeping information private.**

1) Participants should feel safe that any **sensitive information**, **results** or **behaviour** revealed through research won't be discussed with others.

2) Information obtained during a study should remain confidential **unless** the participant agrees it can be shared with others.

3) The study's report shouldn't reveal information or data **identifiable** to an individual.

4) You shouldn't be able to tell who took part or what their individual data was — these should remain **anonymous**.

**Research with non-human animals has caused heated debate.**

1) In **support**, people argue that animal research has provided **valuable information** for psychological and medical research. Some **research designs** couldn't have been conducted on humans — e.g. Harlow did a study which required young monkeys to be separated from their mothers and reared alone.

2) Some **disagree** with the idea of conducting research with non-human animals. They may argue that it's **ethically wrong** to inflict harm and suffering on animals, and obviously animals can't give consent to take part.

3) Some argue that it's cruel to experiment on animals that have a **similar intelligence** to humans, because they might suffer the same problems we would. It'd be OK to experiment on animals that are far less developed than us, but there is no point because they'll be **too different** from us to give results that apply to humans.

## Ethical Guidelines Don't Solve All the Problems

1) There may be researchers who **don't follow the guidelines** properly. Naughty.

2) If a psychologist conducts research in an unacceptable way, they **can't be banned** from research (unlike a doctor who can be 'struck off' for misconduct). But they'd probably be kicked out of their university and the BPS.

3) Even when guidelines are followed, it can be **difficult to assess** things like **psychological harm**, or to **fully justify the use of deception**.

4) Deciding whether the ends (benefits from the study) justify the means (how it was done and at what cost) is not straightforward either. This creates another dilemma for psychologists.

The lasting harm to Milgram's participants was beginning to show.

## Practice Questions

Q1 What does 'informed consent' mean?

Q2 Give one reason why some people think that it is cruel to conduct research on non-human animals.

Q3 For the issue of psychological harm, what level of risk is said to be acceptable in research?

**Exam Question**

Q1 A researcher is carrying out a study of conformity. He has not told the participants the true nature of the research.
   a) Outline one ethical issue caused by this. [2 marks]
   b) Suggest how he could deal with this issue. [2 marks]

## Don't let someone debrief you unless you love them very much...

*Psychological experiments create many ethical dilemmas. Take Milgram's study — there's no doubting that the results reveal interesting things about how people interact. But do these results justify the possible psychological damage done to the participants? There's no right or wrong answer, but the BPS guidelines are there to address exactly this sort of issue.*

# Data Analysis

*Data analysis may sound vaguely maths-like — but don't run for the hills just yet. It isn't too tricky...*

## Data from **Observations** Should be Analysed **Carefully**

1) If you've got **quantitative** data (i.e. numbers), you can use **statistics** to show, for example, the most common behaviours. (Quantitative data can be obtained by **categorising** and **rating** behaviour — see page 12.)

2) **Qualitative** data might consist of a video or audio **recording**, or written **notes** on what the observers witnessed. Analysis of qualitative data is **less straightforward**, but it can still be done.

3) Whatever kind of data you've got, there are some important issues to bear in mind:

   a) There must be **adequate data sampling** to ensure that a **representative** sample of participants' behaviour has been seen.

   b) **Language** must be used **accurately** — the words used to describe behaviour should be **accurate** and **appropriate** (and must have valid **operationalised definitions**). For example, it might not be appropriate to describe a child's behaviour as 'aggressive' if he or she is play-fighting.

   c) Researcher **bias** must be **avoided** — e.g. it's not okay to make notes **only** on events that **support** the researcher's theories, or to have a **biased interpretation** of what is observed.

## The Same Goes for Data Obtained from **Interviews**

1) When **closed** questions are used as part of an interview's structure, **quantitative** data can be produced (e.g. the **number** of participants who replied 'Yes' to a particular question). **Statistics** can then be used (see pages 20-21) to further analyse the data.

2) When **open** questions are used, more **detailed**, **qualitative** data is obtained.

3) Again, whatever you've got, there are certain things you'll need to remember:

   a) **Context** — the **situation** in which a participant said something, and the way they were **behaving** at the time, may be important. It may help the researcher understand **why** something was said, and give clues about the **honesty** of a statement.

   b) The researcher should clearly distinguish **what** was said by the participant from **how** *they* interpreted it.

   c) **Selection** of data — a lot of **qualitative** data may be produced by an interview, which may be difficult for the researcher to **summarise** in a report. The researcher must **avoid** **bias** in selecting what to include (e.g. only including statements that support their ideas). The interviewees may be consulted when deciding **what** to include and **how** to present it.

   d) The interviewer should be aware of how *their* feelings about the interviewee could lead to **biased interpretations** of what they say, or how it is later reported.

## And Likewise for Data from **Questionnaire Surveys**

1) Like observations and interviews, **surveys** can give you both **quantitative** and **qualitative** data, and so most of the points above are relevant to surveys as well.

2) Again, it's especially important to distinguish the **interpretations** of the **researcher** from the **statements** of the **participant**, and to be **unbiased** in selecting what to include in any report on the research.

3) However, the analysis of **written** answers may be especially difficult because the participant is not present to **clarify** any **ambiguities**, plus you don't know the **context** for their answers (e.g. what mood they were in, and so on).

# Data Analysis

## Qualitative *Data Can Be* Tricky *to* Analyse

**Qualitative** data is sometimes seen as 'of **limited use**' because it's difficult to **analyse**.
This is why it's often **converted** into **quantitative** data using **content analysis**.

### CONTENT ANALYSIS

a) A **representative sample** of qualitative data is first **collected** — e.g. from an interview, printed material (newspapers, etc.) or other media (such as TV programmes).

b) **Coding units** are identified to analyse the data. A coding unit could be, for example, an **act of violence**, or the use of **gender stereotypes** (though both of these must be given valid **operationalised definitions** first — e.g. a definition of an 'act of violence').

c) The qualitative data is then **analysed** to see **how often** each coding unit occurs (or **how much** is said about it, etc.).

d) A **statistical analysis** can then be carried out (see pages 20-21).

### ADVANTAGES OF QUANTIFYING DATA

It becomes **easier** to see **patterns** in the data, and easier to **summarise** and **present** it (see pages 24-25).

### DISADVANTAGES OF QUANTIFYING DATA

1) Care is needed to avoid **bias** in defining **coding units**, or deciding which behaviours fit particular units.

2) Qualitative data has **more detail** (**context**, etc.), which is **lost** when it's converted into **numbers**.

1) Because of the **detail** (and hence the **insight**) that **qualitative** data can give, some researchers prefer to **avoid** 'reducing' it to **numbers**.

2) Instead they analyse the data into **categories** or '**typologies**' (e.g. sarcastic remarks, statements about feelings, etc.), **quotations**, **summaries**, and so on.

3) **Hypotheses** may be developed during this analysis, rather than being stated previously, so that they are 'grounded in the data'.

Audrey was disappointed to learn that she'd been reduced to a number.

## Practice Questions

Q1 Distinguish between qualitative and quantitative data.

Q2 Why is data sampling an issue in observation studies?

Q3 Why might survey data be harder to analyse than interview data?

Q4 How is a content analysis done?

**Exam Questions**

Q1 Outline the main differences between qualitative and quantitative data. [4 marks]

Q2 Outline one limitation of collecting quantitative data. [2 marks]

## You must keep an open mind — but just don't let all the facts escape...

*It's fairly obvious-ish, I guess, that qualitative data needs to be analysed with an open mind — it's not OK to fit the facts to your theory... you have to fit your theory to the facts. The same goes for analysing quantitative data — it's not just a case of 'doing some maths' — you have to be sure you're not being biased in your interpretations. Keep that mind open...*

# Descriptive Statistics

*Run for your lives... panic. This really looks like maths... Well, actually, it's not too bad. So calm down.*

## Descriptive Statistics — Just Say What You See...

1) **Descriptive statistics** simply describe the **patterns** found in a set of data.
2) Descriptive statistics uses the fancy term '**central tendency**' to describe an **average**. For example, the central tendency (average) for the height of a group of 18-year-old boys might be about 1.70 metres.

## There are 3 Measures of *Central Tendency* (aka Average) You Need to Know

### The Mean — *This is the 'Normal Average'*

You calculate the **mean** by **adding** all of the scores in a data set and then **dividing** by the number of scores.

$$\text{Mean} = \bar{X} = \frac{\sum X}{N}, \text{ where } \sum X \text{ is the sum of all the scores (and there are } N \text{ of them).}$$

**EXAMPLE:**

If you've got scores of 2, 5, 6, 7 and 10, then...

$\sum X = 30$ (since all the scores add up to 30),

and N = 5 (since there are 5 of them)...

...so the **mean** is $\bar{X} = \dfrac{30}{5} = 6$.

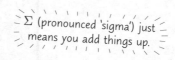
Σ (pronounced 'sigma') just means you add things up.

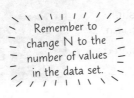
Remember to change N to the number of values in the data set.

**EXAMPLE:**

If you've got scores of 34, 45, 2, 37, 11, 53 and 19, then...

$\sum X = 201$ (since all the scores add up to 201),

and N = 7 (since there are 7 of them)...

...so the mean is $\bar{X} = \dfrac{201}{7} = 28.71$.

**ADVANTAGES:**

a) It uses **all** the scores in a data set.
b) It's used in **further calculations** and so it's handy to work it out.

**DISADVANTAGES:**

a) It can be **skewed** (distorted) by extremely **high** or **low** scores. This can make it **unrepresentative** of most of the scores, and so it may be **misleading**. In these cases, it's best to not use the mean. For example, the scores 10, 40, 25, 20 and 650 have a mean of 149, which is not representative of the central tendency of the data set.
b) It can sometimes give an **unrealistically precise** value (e.g. the average home has 2.4 children — but what does 0.4 of a child mean...?)

# Descriptive Statistics

## The Median — The *Middle Score* When the Data is Put in *Order*

**EXAMPLE:**

The **median** of the scores 4, 5, 10, 12 and 14 is **10**.

In the above example there was **one score** in the **middle**.
If there are **two** middle scores, **add them together** and then **divide by 2** to get the median:

**EXAMPLE:**

The **median** of the scores 2, 6, 27, 45, 52 and 63 is **36**.
In this example there are two middle scores (27 and 45).
So you do,  27 + 45 = 72,  72 ÷ 2 = **36**

**ADVANTAGES:**

a) It's relatively **quick** and **easy** to calculate.

b) It's **not** affected by extremely high or low scores, so it can be used on 'skewed' sets of data to give a '**representative**' average score.

**DISADVANTAGES:**

a) Not **all** the scores are used to work out the median.

b) It has **little further use** in data analysis.

## The Mode — The *Score that Occurs Most Often*

**EXAMPLE:**

The mode (or the modal score) of 2, 5, 2, 9, 6, 11 and 2 is 2.

If there are two scores which are most common then the data set is 'bimodal'. If there are three or more scores which are most common then the data set is 'multimodal'.

**ADVANTAGES:**

a) It shows the **most common** or 'important' score.

b) It's always a result from the actual **data set**, so it can be a more **useful** or **realistic** statistic, e.g. the modal average family has 2 children, not 2.4.

**DISADVANTAGES:**

a) It's not very useful if there are **several** modal values, or if the modal value is only **slightly** more common than other scores.

b) It has **little further use** in data analysis.

## Practice Questions

Q1 Explain how to calculate the mean.
Q2 What is the difference between the mean and the mode?
Q3 How is the median of a data set calculated?

**Exam Questions**

Q1 Work out the mean, median and mode for the following data set: 2, 2, 4, 6, 8, 9, 10. [4 marks]

Q2 Work out the mean, median and mode for the following data set: 12, 7, 8, 19, 5, 7, 19, 22. [4 marks]

## Dame Edna Average — making stats fun, possums...

*These statistics are used to describe a collection of scores in a data set (the middle score, which score occurs most often, and so on), so they're called... wait for it... descriptive statistics. Don't be put off by the weirdy maths notation either — a bar on top of a letter (e.g. $\bar{X}$) means you work out the mean. And a sigma ($\Sigma$) means you add things up. There... not so bad.*

# Correlation

*You know what they say — correlation is as correlation does.*
*Remember that as you read this page... then you won't go far wrong.*

## Correlation Measures How Closely Two Variables are Related

1) **Correlation** is a measure of the relationship between **two variables**, e.g. it can tell you how closely exam grades are related to the amount of revision that someone's done.

2) In a **correlational study** data is collected for some kind of **correlational analysis**.

## The Correlation Coefficient is a Number Between –1 and +1

1) To find the correlation between two variables, you first have to collect some **data**.

   For example, you could ask every student in a class how many hours of study they did each week, and note their average test result.

| Student | Hours of study | Average test score — % |
|---------|----------------|------------------------|
| A | 4 | 58 |
| B | 1 | 23 |
| C | 7 | 67 |
| D | 15 | 89 |

2) You can then work out a **correlation coefficient**. This is a number between –1 and +1, and shows:

   a) **How closely** the variables are linked. This is shown by the **size** of the number — if it's **close** to +1 or –1, then they are **very closely** related, while a smaller number means the relationship is **less strong** (or maybe not there at all if it's close to 0).

   b) The **type** of correlation — a **positive** correlation coefficient (i.e. between 0 and +1) means that the variables rise and fall together, while a negative correlation coefficient (i.e. between –1 and 0) means that as one variable rises, the other falls. (See below for more info.)

## Correlation is Easy to See on Scatter Graphs

1) **Positive correlation** — this means that as one variable rises, so does the other (and likewise, if one falls, so does the other).

   Example: hours of study and average test score.

   The correlation coefficient is roughly **0.75** (close to +1).

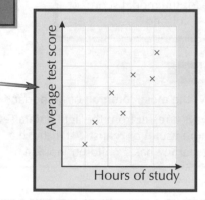

2) **Negative correlation** — this means that as one variable rises, the other one falls (and vice versa).

   Example: hours of TV watched each week and average test score. The correlation coefficient is roughly **–0.75** (close to -1).

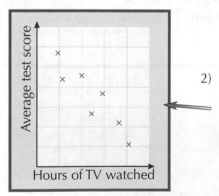

3) **No correlation** — if the correlation coefficient is 0 (or close to 0), then the two variables aren't linked.

   Example: a student's height and their average test score.

   The correlation coefficient is roughly **0.01** (close to 0).

# Correlation

## Correlational Research has some Advantages...

1) Because correlational research doesn't involve **controlling** any variables, you can do it
   when (for **practical** or **ethical** reasons) you couldn't do a **controlled experiment**. Handy.

> For example, an experiment into the effects of smoking on humans probably
> wouldn't be done for ethical reasons, but a correlation between smoking and
> cancer could be established from hospital records.

2) Correlational analysis can give ideas for **future** research (e.g. physiological research on the effects of smoking).

3) Correlation can even be used to test for **reliability** and **validity** (e.g. by testing the results of the same test taken
   twice by the same people — a good **reliable** test will show a **high correlation**).

## ...but some Limitations

1) Correlational analysis **can't** establish 'cause and effect' relationships
   — it can only show that there's a **statistical link** between the variables.

   Variables can be closely correlated without changes in one causing
   changes in the other — a **third variable** could be involved. Only a
   **controlled experiment** can show cause and effect relationships.

   > For example, the number of births in a town was found to be positively
   > correlated to the number of storks that nested in that town — but that didn't
   > mean that more storks caused the increase. (It was because more people in the
   > town led to more births, and also to more houses with chimneys to nest on.)

2) Care must be taken when **interpreting** correlation coefficients
   — high correlation coefficients could be down to **chance**.

## Practice Questions

Q1 Explain what is meant by correlation.

Q2 What is a correlation coefficient?

Q3 What two things are shown by a correlation coefficient?

Q4 Explain the difference between a negative correlation and no correlation.

**Exam Questions**

Q1 a) A study has found a negative correlation between tiredness and reaction time.
Explain what this means. [2 marks]

   b) Another psychologist is studying the effect of heart rate on reaction time.
   His results are shown in the scattergraph to the right.

   Use the scattergraph to describe the relationship
   between heart rate and reaction time in this study. [4 marks]

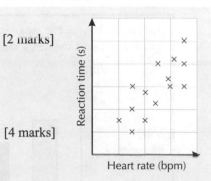

## Stats sucks...

*Look at the graphs showing the large positive and large negative correlations — all the points lie close-ish to a straight line,
which slopes either upwards (positive correlation) or downwards (negative correlation). Don't worry if the points on your
scatter graph are all a-mish-mash with no pattern whatsoever. It just means that you can say that your variables aren't linked.
Now, hours spent doing statistics and amount of fun — hmmm....what sort of correlation would that show I wonder...*

# Summarising the Data

*Ahhh graphs... It's not very scientific or anything, but the only bit about statistics I don't find mind-numbingly boring is the bit where you get to make all the numbers look nice and pretty and colourful... it's just lovely.*

## Data Can Be Presented in Various Ways

1) **Qualitative** data from observations, interviews, surveys, etc. (see pages 6-7) can be presented in a **report** as a **'verbal summary'**.

2) The report would contain **summaries** of what was seen or said, possibly using **categories** to group data together. Also **quotations** from participants can be used, and any **research hypotheses** that developed during the study or data analysis may be discussed.

3) When **quantitative** data is **collected** (or **produced** from the data, e.g. by a **content analysis** — see page 19), it can be **summarised** and presented in various ways. Read on...

## Tables are a Good Way to Summarise Quantitative Data

**Tables** can be used to clearly present the data and show any **patterns** in the scores.

Tables of **'raw data'** show the scores **before** any **analysis** has been done on them.

Other tables may show **descriptive statistics** such as the mean, mode and median (see pages 20-21).

*Edward's data was summarised nicely on his table.*

### Table To Show the Qualities of Different Types of Ice Cream

| Type of ice cream | Quality (score out of 10) | | |
| --- | --- | --- | --- |
| | Tastiness | Thickness | Throwability |
| Chocolate | 9 | 7 | 6 |
| Toffee | 8 | 6 | 7 |
| Strawberry | 8 | 5 | 4 |
| Earwax | 2 | 9 | 8 |

## Bar Charts Can be Used for Non-continuous Data

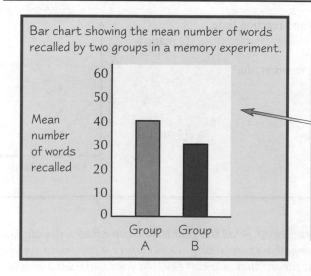

Bar chart showing the mean number of words recalled by two groups in a memory experiment.

**Bar charts** (bar graphs) are usually used to present **'non-continuous data'** (like when a variable falls into **categories** rather than being measured on a numbered scale).

This bar chart shows the mean number of words recalled by different groups in a memory experiment.

Note that the columns in bar charts **don't touch** each other. Also, it's preferable to always show the **full vertical scale**, or **clearly indicate** when it isn't all shown (otherwise it can be **misleading**).

# Summarising the Data

*Nearly done — just a little bit more...*

## Histograms are for When You Have Continuous Data

Histograms show data measured on a 'continuous' scale of measurement.

This histogram shows the time different participants took to complete a task.

Each column shows a **class interval** (here, each class interval is 10 seconds), and the columns **touch** each other.

It's the **height** of the column that shows the number of values in that interval. (**All** intervals are shown, even if there are **no scores** within them.)

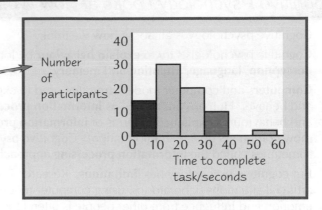

## Frequency Polygons are Good for Showing More Than One Set of Data

**Frequency polygons** are similar to histograms, but use **lines** to show where the top of each column would reach.

It can be useful to combine **two or more** frequency polygons on the same set of axes — then it's easy to **make comparisons** between groups.

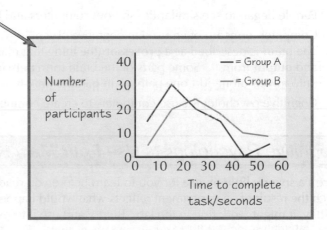

## Practice Questions

Q1  What kind of information is typically shown in tables?

Q2  What kind of data is shown on bar charts?

Q3  What type of data do histograms represent?

Q4  What advantage do frequency polygons have over histograms?

### Exam Questions

Q1  Sketch a frequency polygon of the data in the table on page 24.    [4 marks]

Q2  What can be concluded from the bar chart on page 24?    [2 marks]

## What goes 'Graph graph graph'? A dog with a sore throat...*

*Right. One section down. That lot should have given you a bit of background about how psychologists conduct research, which will be pretty helpful to you while you're reading the rest of this book. And if along the way you find yourself asking "What's a repeated measures design?" or "What's opportunity sampling?" you can always flick back and have another read.*

* Or a crowd at a senior's tennis match. Or a maths teacher.
  Or my dad coughing in the morning. Or... oh think of your own...

# The Cognitive Approach

*Here we go with Cognitive Psychology. If you're just having a flick through and weren't actually thinking about work just yet — too late. Grab a ticket and climb aboard the revision train, cos it's non-stop all the way to Examsville...*

## Cognitive Psychology Looks at How We *Interpret* the World

1) Cognitive psychology is all about **how** we think.

2) Cognitive psychologists try to **explain behaviour** by looking at our **perception**, **language**, **attention** and **memory**.

You've been experiencing downtime due to access problems with your communication software. I'll need to back-up your hard drive and then reboot you. Simple.

3) **Computers** and computer models are often used to explain how we think and behave. Humans are treated as **information processors** (computers) and behaviour is explained in terms of **information processing** (how computers deal with information). Cognitive psychology is sometimes called the **information processing** approach.

4) But cognitive psychology has **limitations**. Research is often carried out in artificial situations (laboratories, using computer models) and the role of emotion and influence from other people is often ignored. For these reasons some argue that the results aren't valid in the real world.

5) A second criticism is that cognitive psychology fails to take **individual differences** into account by assuming that all of us process stuff in exactly the same way.

## Cognitive Psychology Developed as the *Computer Age Developed*

1) People began to see similarities in how computers and humans make sense of information.

2) Computer terms are often used in cognitive psychology:
The brain is described as a **processor** (the thing that makes things happen) — it has data **input** into it, and **output** from it. Some parts of the brain form **networks** (connections of bits). Other parts work in **serial** (info travels along just one path) or in **parallel** (info travels to and fro along lots of paths at the same time).

3) Cognitive psychologists use computers to create **computational models** of the human mind.

## Cognitive Psychologists Use *Four* Main Research Methods

Here's a snappy little phrase for you to learn before you read on: '**ecological validity**' — it's the measure of how much the result of an experiment reflects what would happen in **natural settings**. If a result has **low** ecological validity, it might work fine in the lab. But try and use it to explain real life behaviour, and you'll find yourself up the creek without a paddle. And no-one wants that.

### 1 — Laboratory Experiments

A lot of research in cognitive psychology happens in **laboratories**. This is very **scientific** and reliable as it is possible to have great control over variables in a lab. However, often this type of research doesn't tell us much about the real world — it has **low ecological validity**.

### 2 — Field Experiments

**Field experiments** take place in a **natural** situation (e.g. studies of memory or attention in a school environment), so they have more ecological validity, but there's less control of other variables.

### 3 — Natural Experiments

Natural experiments involve making observations of a **naturally occurring situation**. The experimenter has little control of the variables, and participants can't be randomly assigned to conditions. Natural experiments have **high ecological validity**, but they're **not massively reliable**, as **uncontrolled** (or **confounding**) variables can affect the results.

### 4 — Brain Imaging

**Brain imaging** can now be carried out during a cognitive task. For example, MRI scans have been used to show the blood flow in different brain areas for different types of memory tasks.

# The Cognitive Approach

## Case Studies *Provide Support for the Cognitive Approach*

Case studies use patients' behaviour to test a theory. **Brain damaged** patients are often studied — the damaged parts of the brain are linked to observed differences in behaviour. However, it's hard to make **generalisations** from the study of subjects with brain damage to 'normal' individuals. Also, **individual differences** between people mean that one subject may respond in a way that is totally different from someone else. Hmmm, tricky.

Cognitive psychologists believe that the different types of memory are **separate systems** in the brain. The case study of HM supported this by showing that short- and long-term memory must be based in different brain structures.

### Milner et al (1957) — case study of HM

| | |
|---|---|
| **Diagnosis:** | HM was a patient with severe and frequent epilepsy. His seizures were based in a brain structure called the hippocampus. In 1953, doctors decided to surgically remove part of the brain round this area. |
| **Results:** | The operation reduced his epilepsy, but led to him suffering memory loss.<br>He could still form short-term memories (STMs), but was unable to form new long-term memories (LTMs). For example, he could read something over and over without realising that he had read it before. He also moved house and had difficulty recalling the new route to his house. However, he could still talk and show previous skills (**procedural memory**). From tests, they found HM's **episodic memory** (for past events) and **semantic memory** (for knowledge, e.g. word meanings) was affected more than his **procedural memory**. |

## Cognitive Psychologists Apply *Animal Research* to Humans

The results of **non-human** studies can be **applied** to human cognitive abilities. For example, discovering whether chimpanzees can learn language helps psychologists develop theories about how humans learn language.

However, there are so many **differences** between humans and animals that results can be explained wrongly. For example, you might conclude that chimpanzees can't learn a **spoken** language because they lack the **cognitive** abilities. But it's actually more likely to be because they lack the **physiological** attributes, like a voice box.

I know the following study doesn't really generalise to humans, but you need to know about it.

OCR Core Study

### Savage-Rumbaugh (1986) — symbol communication in chimps

| | |
|---|---|
| **Method:** | Two pygmy chimpanzees and two common chimpanzees were taught to communicate using symbols on a keyboard. A mixture of training and observation of others was used. All communications were recorded. |
| **Results:** | Common chimps needed training to form symbol-object associations. However, pygmy chimps spontaneously used symbols to communicate after observing others. The pygmy chimps were also able to understand and respond to spoken English, unlike the common chimps. |
| **Conclusion:** | Two closely related species differ greatly in their ability to develop a symbolic communication system. |
| **Evaluation:** | There are **ethical** considerations, in that the chimps were taken from their natural environment and taught to do something that was extremely unnatural to them. There are also issues of **external validity** — it's not possible to accurately generalise results from chimpanzees to humans. |

## Practice Questions

Q1 Why is cognitive psychology sometimes called the information processing approach?

Q2 Why are laboratory experiments more reliable than field experiments?

Q3 How is brain imaging useful in cognitive psychology?

**Exam Questions**

| | | |
|---|---|---|
| Q1 | Outline one assumption of the cognitive approach in psychology. | [2 marks] |
| Q2 | Give one disadvantage of animal research in cognitive psychology. | [2 marks] |

## Syntax error. Funny line does not compute. Insert file 'humour for books'.

*If your brain goes wrong just turn it off and on again. That normally works for me. One day we'll probably know enough about the brain to be able to build computer people. Then you could make a computerised version of yourself and amaze your friends and family by projecting illegally downloaded TV out of your own face. Imagine that. They'd be so proud...*

# Eyewitness Testimony

*If you witness a crime or an accident, you might have to report what you saw, and your version of events could be crucial in prosecuting someone... But your memory isn't as accurate as you might think...*

## Eyewitness Testimony Can Be **Inaccurate** and **Distorted**

1) **Eyewitness testimony** (EWT) is the **evidence** provided by people who **witnessed** a particular event or crime. It relies on **recall** from memory.

2) EWT includes, for example, **descriptions** of criminals (e.g. hair colour, height) and crime scenes (e.g. time, date, location).

3) Witnesses are often **inaccurate** in their recollection of events and the people involved. As you can probably imagine, this has important implications when it comes to police interviews.

4) Many cognitive psychologists focus on working out what **factors** affect the accuracy of eyewitness testimony, and how accuracy can be **improved** in interviews.

## Eyewitness Testimony Can Be Affected by **Misleading Information**

**Loftus and Palmer (1974)** investigated how EWT can be **distorted**.
They used **leading questions**, where a certain answer is subtly implied in the question:

### Loftus and Palmer (1974) studied eyewitness testimony.

Loftus and Palmer carried out two experiments in their study.

**Experiment 1:**

| | |
|---|---|
| **Method:** | Participants were shown a film of a multiple car crash. They were then asked a series of questions including 'How fast do you think the cars were going when they **hit**?' In different conditions, the word 'hit' was replaced with '**smashed**', '**collided**', '**bumped**' or '**contacted**'. |
| **Results:** | It was seen that participants given the word '**smashed**' estimated the **highest speed** (an average of 41 mph), and those given the word '**contacted**' gave the **lowest** estimate (an average of 32 mph). |

**Experiment 2:**

| | |
|---|---|
| **Method:** | The participants were split into three groups. One group was given the verb 'smashed', another 'hit', and the third, control group wasn't given any indication of the vehicles' speed. A week later, the participants were asked '**Did you see any broken glass?**'. |
| **Results:** | Although there was no broken glass in the film, participants were more likely to say that they'd seen broken glass in the '**smashed**' condition than any other. |
| **Conclusion:** | **Leading questions** can affect the **accuracy** of people's memories of an event. |
| **Evaluation:** | This has implications for questions in **police interviews**. However, this was an artificial experiment — watching a video is not as **emotionally arousing** as a real-life event, which potentially affects recall. In fact, a later study found that participants who thought they'd witnessed a **real** robbery gave a more **accurate** description of the robber. The experimental design might lead to **demand characteristics**, where the results are skewed because of the participants' expectations about the purposes of the experiment. For example, the leading questions might have given participants **clues** about the nature of the experiment (e.g. they could have realised that the experiment was about susceptibility to leading questions), and so participants might have acted accordingly. This would have reduced the **validity** and **reliability** of the experiment. |

# Eyewitness Testimony

## Loftus and Zanni (1975) also Looked at Leading Questions

Loftus and Zanni (1975) investigated how altering the wording of a question can produce a **leading question** that can distort EWT.

### Loftus and Zanni (1975) studied leading questions.

| | |
|---|---|
| **Method:** | Participants were shown a film of a car crash. They were then asked either 'Did you see **the** broken headlight?' or 'Did you see **a** broken headlight?'. There was no broken headlight shown in the film. |
| **Results:** | Even though there was no broken headlight, 7% of those asked about 'a' broken headlight claimed they saw one, compared to 17% in the group asked about 'the' broken headlight. |
| **Conclusion:** | The simple use of the word 'the' is enough to affect the accuracy of people's memories of an event. |
| **Evaluation:** | Like the study by Loftus and Palmer (see previous page), this study has implications for eyewitness testimony. This study was a **laboratory study**, which made it possible to control any **extraneous variables**. This means it's possible to establish **cause and effect**. However, the study was **artificial** (participants were shown a film of a car crash, not an actual car crash), so the study lacked **ecological validity**. |

## The Age of the Witness can Affect the Accuracy of Eyewitness Testimony

Studies have shown that the **age** of the witness can have an effect on the accuracy of eyewitness testimony.

### Valentine and Coxon (1997) studied the effect of age on EWT.

| | |
|---|---|
| **Method:** | 3 groups of participants (children, young adults and elderly people) watched a video of a kidnapping. They were then asked a series of leading and non-leading questions about what they had seen. |
| **Results:** | Both the elderly people and the children gave more incorrect answers to non-leading questions. Children were misled more by leading questions than adults or the elderly. |
| **Conclusion:** | Age has an effect on the accuracy of eyewitness testimony. |
| **Evaluation:** | This has **implications** in law when children or elderly people are questioned. However, the experiment was **artificial** and so wasn't as emotionally arousing as the same situation would have been in real life — the study **lacks external validity**. The study could have seemed like an experiment into how well people remember things from **TV**, which isn't the same as real life. |

## Practice Questions

Q1  What is eyewitness testimony?

Q2  What are leading questions?

Q3  Give one factor that can affect the accuracy of eyewitness testimony.

**Exam Question**

Q1  From experiment 1 of the study of Loftus and Palmer:
- a)  Briefly describe the method used.                                      [2 marks]
- b)  Give one limitation of the method used in the experiment.             [2 marks]

## Do you remember the fun time you had reading this page...?*

If you witness something dead important, remember that not everything you think you remember did definitely happen. Leading questions can, for example, mislead people into thinking they saw something they didn't. This is especially true in children. So little brother, what colour was the dog that you saw eating all Mum's luxury chocolate biscuits? Burp.

*...or will you not be fooled by a leading question?

# Eyewitness Testimony

*Two more pages on eyewitness testimony coming up — bet you're as excited as I am...*

## Anxiety *Can Affect* Focus

Psychologists tend to believe that **small increases** in anxiety and arousal may **increase the accuracy** of memory, but **high levels** have a **negative effect** on accuracy.

In **violent crimes** (where anxiety and arousal are likely to be high), the witness may focus on **central details** (e.g. a weapon) and neglect other peripheral details (e.g. what the criminal was wearing).

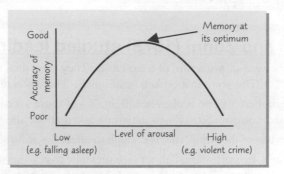

Eyewitnesses recall seeing a large, threatening candle, but nothing else remarkable.

### Loftus (1979) studied weapon focus in EWT.

| | |
|---|---|
| **Method:** | In a study with an **independent groups** design, participants heard a discussion in a nearby room. In one condition, a man came out of the room with a pen and grease on his hands. In the second condition, the man came out carrying a knife covered in blood. Participants were asked to identify the man from 50 photographs. |
| **Results:** | Participants in condition 1 were 49% accurate. Only 33% of the participants in condition 2 were correct. |
| **Conclusion:** | When anxious and aroused, witnesses focus on a weapon at the expense of other details. |
| **Evaluation:** | The study has **high ecological validity**, as the participants weren't aware that the study was staged. However, this means that there are also **ethical** considerations, as participants could have been very distressed at the sight of the man with the knife. |

## Reconstructive Memory *Can Play a Part in EWT*

1)  Reconstructive memory is about filling the gaps in our memories.
2)  **Bartlett** believed that when we remember something, we only store **some** elements of the experience.
3)  We **reconstruct** events using these elements, filling in the **gaps** in the memory with our own **schemas**, to form **reconstructive memories**.
4)  Schemas are **ready-stored opinions** and **expectations** which we use for quick judgements to deal with the world.

### Bartlett (1932) demonstrated reconstructive memory.

| | |
|---|---|
| **Method:** | Participants were shown a short story from a different culture, which therefore contained **unfamiliar** material. Participants were asked to **recall** the story several different times over a number of days. |
| **Results:** | The recalled stories were always **shorter** than the original. Many parts were recalled from the participants' own cultural perspectives, with certain facts **changed** to fit. For example, 'canoe' was changed to 'boat'. The recalled version soon became very **fixed** over time with only minor variations. |
| **Conclusion:** | The **meaning** of a story is remembered, but the gaps are filled in with more familiar material to make the story **easier** to remember. This has an effect of **skewing** (shaping) information to make it fit our schemas. |
| **Comment:** | It is possible that errors occurred from **conscious guessing** rather than participants actually believing that their recalled stories were the same as the original. Later studies have found that if participants were told from the beginning that **accurate recall** was required, errors dropped significantly. |

# Eyewitness Testimony

## The **Cognitive Interview** was Developed to **Increase Accuracy**

Cognitive psychologists have played a big part in helping to **increase the accuracy** of eyewitness testimony. As you've seen, research shows that the accuracy of eyewitness testimony is affected by many factors. The **cognitive interview technique** was developed by **Geiselman et al (1984)** to try to increase the accuracy of witnesses' recall of events during police questioning.

Here's basically what happens in cognitive interviews:

1) The interviewer tries to make the witness **relaxed** and tailors his/her **language** to suit the witness.
2) The witness recreates the environmental and internal (e.g. mood) **context** of the crime scene.
3) The witness reports absolutely **everything** that they can remember about the crime.
4) The witness is asked to recall details of the crime in **different orders**.
5) The witness is asked to recall the event from various **different perspectives**, e.g. from the eyes of other witnesses.
6) The interviewer avoids any **judgemental** and **personal comments**.

## There is **Research** to **Support** the Cognitive Interview

Research has shown that people interviewed with the cognitive interview technique are much more **accurate** in their recall of events. For example:

### Geiselman et al (1986) studied the effect of the cognitive interview.

| | |
|---|---|
| **Method:** | In a staged situation, an intruder carrying a **blue** rucksack entered a classroom and stole a slide projector. Two days later, participants were questioned about the event. The study used an **independent groups** design — participants were either questioned using a standard interview procedure or the cognitive interview technique. Early in the questioning, participants were asked 'Was the guy with the **green** backpack nervous?'. Later in the interview, participants were asked what colour the man's rucksack was. |
| **Results:** | Participants in the cognitive interview condition were less likely to recall the rucksack as being green than those in the standard interview condition. |
| **Conclusion:** | The cognitive interview technique **enhances memory recall** and **reduces the effect of leading questions**. |
| **Evaluation:** | The experiment was conducted as though a real crime had taken place in the classroom — it had **high ecological validity**. The experiment used an **independent groups** design (see page 10). The disadvantage of this is that the participants in the cognitive interview condition could have been naturally less susceptible to leading questions than the other group. |

## Practice Questions

Q1 How do high levels of anxiety affect memory?

Q2 How can schemas affect the accuracy of memory?

Q3 Give an example of a study that supports the use of the cognitive interview.

**Exam Question**

Q1 Discuss the strengths and limitations of the cognitive approach in psychology using examples from studies of your choice.

[12 marks]

## A tall thin man, quite short, with black, fair hair — great fat bloke she was...

*Well, now I haven't a clue what I've really experienced in my life. Did that man I saw shoplifting really have stubble, scars, a pierced chin and a ripped leather jacket, or is that just my shoplifter stereotype kicking in? In fact, come to think of it, I couldn't actually tell you whether my granny has a hairy chin or not. I think she does, but then I think all grannies do...*

# Variations in Cognitive Performance

*We're not all equally good at everything — that'd be boring. Cognitive performance can differ between people because of disorders (e.g. autism and Asperger syndrome) and because of individual differences.*

## People with **Autism** Have Communicative, Social and Linguistic Problems

1) A person with autism will tend to have the following characteristics:

   - Be **withdrawn** and poor at forming relationships.
   - Be less likely to **respond** to environmental stimuli, especially people.
   - Have **communication difficulties**, such as abnormal speech.
   - Have **compulsive** and **ritualistic behaviour**, including an obsession with **sameness**.

2) **Very occasionally**, people with autism are **exceptionally gifted**, in areas such as music, mathematics and art.

3) There are thought to be two types of autism:

   a) The **Asperger** type (**Asperger syndrome**) tend to have normal or above normal intelligence and some neurological problems (e.g. motor difficulties).

   b) The **Kanner** type tend to have **learning disabilities** and additional **problems**, such as epilepsy.

## Someone with Autism may **Lack a "Theory of Mind"**

1) A **theory of mind** is our understanding that other people see the world in **different ways** from us.

2) **Very young children** don't have theory of mind — they don't understand that other people think or see things differently.

3) To have a social or emotional **relationship** with another person, it's important to understand their different emotional state or point of view — you need to have a theory of mind.

4) If autistic children don't develop a theory of mind, it may explain why they may find **social contact** difficult.

The chocolate cake was Amy's — she didn't care what anyone else's point of view was.

### Baron-Cohen et al (1985) studied theory of mind in autistic children.

**Method:** Three groups of children were studied — children with autism with an average age of 12 years, children with Down Syndrome with an average age of 11 years, and 'normal' children with an average age of 4 years. The experimenter had two dolls, Sally and Anne. Sally had a basket, Anne a box. Children were asked to name the dolls (the **naming question**). Then Sally was seen to hide a marble in her basket and leave the room. Anne took the marble and put it in her box. Sally returned and the child was asked, 'Where will Sally look for her marble?' (**belief question**). The correct response is to point to the basket, where Sally believes the marble to be. They were also asked, 'Where is the marble really?' (**reality question**) and 'Where was the marble in the beginning?' (**memory question**). Each child was tested twice, with the marble in a different place the second time.

**Results:** **100%** of the children got the **naming** question, **reality** question and **memory** question correct. In the **belief** question, the children with Down Syndrome scored **86%**, the 'normal' children **85%**, but the children with autism scored **20%**.

**Conclusion:** The results were not due to **learning disabilities**, as both the autistic children and those with Down Syndrome had similar mental ages. The findings therefore seem to suggest that autistic children have **under-developed theories of mind**. They seem unable to predict or understand the beliefs of others.

**Evaluation:** Dolls were used throughout the study, causing it to lack **ecological validity**. Also, as **dolls** were used, it may be that children with autism had a more highly developed theory of mind and understood that dolls did not have beliefs. Repeating the study by acting out the scenes with **humans** might show an increase in ability on theory of mind tasks. However, when **Leslie and Frith (1988)** did a similar study with real people and not dolls, the same pattern of results was obtained.

# Variations in Cognitive Performance

## Asperger Syndrome is a Form of Autism

1) A person with Asperger syndrome will tend to have the following characteristics:

- difficulties with social interaction.
- communication difficulties, e.g. difficulty understanding gestures, facial expressions and tones of voice.
- narrow interests, and a preoccupation with them.
- motor difficulties (clumsiness).

Baron-Cohen followed the traditional dress of his family on his days off.

2) Unlike the Kanner type of autism, people with Asperger syndrome:
- don't have language difficulties,
- don't have a delay in their cognitive development.

## Some Research has Focused on Adults with Autism or Asperger Syndrome

Although a lot of work is focused on theory of mind in children, some studies explore theory of mind in adults.

### Baron-Cohen et al (1997) studied theory of mind in adults.

*OCR Core Study*

**Method:** The researchers tested theory of mind ability in adults with high-functioning autism or Asperger syndrome. People with autism or Asperger syndrome aren't usually able to reason about what another person thinks. However, people with high-functioning autism or Asperger syndrome can do this. Participants were given photographs of faces with just the eyes showing and were asked to assess the person's mental state. Two control tasks were also used — recognising a person's gender from a photograph of their eyes, and recognising basic emotions from a whole face. The experiment used a repeated measures design (see page 10) — all participants did all the tasks. Two control groups were used — age-matched normal controls and a group with Tourette's syndrome.

**Results:** It was seen that participants with high-functioning autism or Asperger syndrome were significantly impaired at inferring a person's mental state. However, they were unimpaired on both control tasks.

**Conclusion:** Individuals with high-functioning autism or Asperger syndrome are impaired on a subtle theory of mind test.

**Evaluation:** The use of control tasks and control groups allowed the researchers to make comparisons with their results. Although the test is an advanced test of theory of mind, it's still much simpler than the demands of interaction and communication in everyday life. The stimuli are still photographs — the real world is hardly ever still. Gestures and expressions happen very quickly with little time for interpretation. A better set of stimuli would therefore be film clips, which would better represent real life and improve the study's ecological validity.

## Practice Questions

Q1 Describe the characteristics of someone with autism.

Q2 Name the two types of autism.

Q3 What is a 'theory of mind'?

Q4 Describe the characteristics of someone with Asperger syndrome.

**Exam Questions**

Q1 Outline the method of Baron-Cohen et al's (1997) study. [4 marks]

Q2 Describe one limitation of Baron-Cohen et al's (1997) study. How could this have been overcome? [4 marks]

## One thing's for sure — you're gonna need a theory of psychology...

*As you've probably noticed, there's another Core Study on this page — you can probably expect to get a question on it in your exam. So, make sure you know what the researchers did and what they found out. And just to top it all off, make sure you've got a few evaluation points up your magical psychology sleeve to pull out at the appropriate moment.*

# The Developmental Approach

*Developmental psychologists focus on how we change and develop throughout our lives. Describing **how** we change isn't enough though — they also try to explain **why** the changes take place. Show-offs.*

## Different **Research Methods** Are Used **Depending** On What's Being Studied

(There's more general stuff on research methods on pages 6-7, for those of you who can't get enough of 'em...)

### Observational Studies Can Be Naturalistic or Controlled

1) **Naturalistic observation** takes place in the child's own environment and none of the variables are manipulated — e.g. a parent might note down their child's behaviour in a diary.

| Advantage | Disadvantage |
|---|---|
| **Ecological validity** — behaviour will be natural because the subject is in a real-life, familiar setting. | **Extraneous variables** — there's no control over the variables, so you can't be sure what caused your results. |

2) With **controlled observation** the child is observed by a researcher, usually in a laboratory setting. Some of the variables are controlled — e.g. a child might be given a certain toy to play with and observed through a one-way mirror, like in Bandura et al's study (see page 39).

| Advantage | Disadvantage |
|---|---|
| **Control** — the effect of **extraneous variables** is minimised, so you're more likely to be able to establish cause and effect. | **Observer bias** — the observer's expectations may affect what they focus on and record, so the reliability of the results might be a problem. Another observer might have come up with very different results. |

### Correlational Studies Look for Relationships Between Variables

**Variables** often rise and fall together — e.g. height and weight usually rise together as a child grows. But this doesn't mean that one variable **causes** the other to change — that's pretty important to remember. The data for correlational studies often comes from surveys, questionnaires and interviews.

| Advantage | Disadvantage |
|---|---|
| **Ethical** — you can study variables that would be unethical to manipulate, e.g. whether there's a relationship between smoking during pregnancy and low birthweight. | **Causal relationships** — these can't be assumed from a correlation. Results may be caused by a third, unknown variable. |

### Case Studies Are Detailed Descriptions of One Person

**Case studies** allow researchers to analyse unusual cases in lots of detail — e.g. Freud's study of **Little Hans** (page 37).

| Advantage | Disadvantage |
|---|---|
| **Rich data** — researchers have the opportunity to study rare phenomena in a lot of detail. | **Generalisation** — only using a single case makes generalising the results extremely difficult. |

### Interviews Are like Conversations

1) **Clinical interviews** are used loads in developmental psychology. They're **semi-structured**, meaning that the researcher asks some specific questions, but also lets the participant ramble on about stuff.
2) Participants could be children, or their carers, teachers or parents.
3) Face-to-face interviews can include **open-ended** (non-specific) or **fixed** (specific) questions.

| Advantage | Disadvantage |
|---|---|
| **Rich data** — especially from open-ended questions. | **Participants** — children can have implicit knowledge but be unable to verbalise it, so their skills can be underestimated. |

# The Developmental Approach

## Experiments Can Have a Longitudinal or Cross-Sectional Design

Two main kinds of experimental design are used to work out how behaviour changes with age
— **longitudinal** and **cross-sectional**. These are used **alongside** the **research method**.

1) A **longitudinal design** tests the **same people** repeatedly as they get older and wrinklier.

2) This means you can plot the **group average** as a function of age. It also allows you to look at the development of **individuals** within the group.

3) Researchers can then look at whether the data shows a **gradual change**, or a more sudden shift that suggests **stage-like development**.

4) Longitudinal designs can be **retrospective**. This involves looking back over a period of time — e.g. looking at a child's medical history.

**Advantage** — you get detailed data about the same people, and individual differences are taken into account.

**Disadvantage** — studying the development of the same people can take years, so it's time-consuming and costly.

1) A **cross-sectional design** tests different people of **different ages**. For example, if you wanted to look at how vocabulary increases with age, you could measure the vocabulary of children in different year groups.

2) Their performance is then **averaged** over different individuals at each age.

**Advantage** — they provide a quick estimate of developmental changes, and are much less time-consuming than a longitudinal design.

**Disadvantage** — they don't take individual differences into account. Different people are measured at each age, so you can't be sure they all developed in the same way.

## Researchers Have to Think About Ethics

Psychologists have to be extra careful when they're conducting research with children.

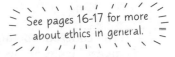
See pages 16-17 for more about ethics in general.

1) Under-16s might not understand the implications of participating in a study, so researchers have to get **informed consent** from their parents or guardians.

2) It's important that researchers get the **power balance** right because children generally view adults as more powerful than them. Extra care has to be taken to inform children of their rights — e.g. the right to **withdraw**.

3) Researchers need to make sure that a study won't cause the participants physical or psychological **harm**. They have to use the **least stressful** procedure possible, and **abandon** the study if the child seems distressed.

**Animal studies** have provided **valuable information** for developmental research. But there's debate about whether they're ethical or not.

**Advantage** — Some **research designs** couldn't have been conducted on humans ethically.

**Disadvantages** — Some see it as **unethical** to inflict suffering on animals, especially when they can't give consent. Animals and humans are different, so you can't **generalise** results from one species to the other.

## Practice Questions

Q1 Give one advantage of correlational studies.

Q2 Give one disadvantage of longitudinal designs.

Q3 What ethical considerations are important when children are involved in a study?

**Exam Question**

Q1 a) Identify a research method used in the developmental approach. [2 marks]

b) Evaluate the research method you identified in part a). [4 marks]

## I once did an experiment on my luggage...*

Basically there are loads of different ways to test your theory, so all you need to do is pick the one that best fits whatever you're studying. Or you could just shut your eyes, point at the page, and see what comes up. A word of advice though — if you end up trying to do clinical interviews on babies, then maybe have a rethink. Or try monkeys instead...

* It was a case study.

# Theories of Child Development

*Things are going to get theory-tastic now, so strap yourself in and prepare for take-off...*

## Piaget's Theory is the Most **Well Known** Theory of **Cognitive Development**

A child's mental abilities and skills develop with time — things like paying attention, learning, thinking and remembering. But as with so much in psychology, there are loads of theories to explain how this happens.

### *Piaget suggested four major stages of cognitive development*

1. The **sensorimotor stage** (birth to 2 years) — At first, a child only performs simple **reflex** activities such as sucking. Gradually, through repetition, the child learns more complex routines. After about 8 months, the child has **object permanence** — it realises that objects continue to exist even when it can't see them. At about 18 months, the child shows **representational thought** — it searches for missing objects (showing that it can think about things that it can't see), and shows the beginnings of language.

2. The **pre-operational stage** (2 to 7 years) — The child starts **constructing** and **using** mental symbols (e.g. language) to think about **situations**, **objects** and **events**. However, it can't **conserve** — it can't understand that the properties of something don't change if its appearance changes (e.g. that there's still the same amount of liquid even if it's poured into a taller glass). Piaget thought that children at this stage hadn't yet acquired the ability to **think logically**, hence this is the **pre**-operational stage. Piaget divided the pre-operational stage into:

    a) The **pre-conceptual period** (2 to 4 years) — The child shows **animism** (assigning qualities of living things to non-living things), **transductive reasoning** (concentrating only on one aspect to work something out, e.g. if a car has wheels, and a random thing has wheels, then that thing must be a car) and **egocentrism** (only viewing the world from their own perspective).

    b) The **intuitive period** (4 to 7 years) — The child becomes **less egocentric** and better at classifying objects due to their perceptual attributes, e.g. size, colour.

3. The **concrete operational stage** (7 to 11 years) — The child learns **new ways of thinking** about **new objects**, **events** and **situations**. It can **conserve** and think **logically**, but only about **real** situations.

4. The **formal operational stage** (11 years and up) — The child is now able to think about **abstract** ideas (e.g. 'justice'). It can also think about **hypothetical** events.

## *Samuel and Bryant tested Piaget's theory of conservation*

In Piaget's standard conservation task, children are shown two rows of counters, each with the same number, and asked if each row contains the same amount of counters. Then one row is spread out, and they're asked the question again. Samuel and Bryant investigated whether younger children fail Piaget's conservation task because they think that if a question's asked twice, then two different answers are required.

### Samuel and Bryant (1984) varied conservation tasks.

| | |
|---|---|
| **Method:** | Samuel and Bryant carried out a **laboratory experiment** with an **independent groups** design. 252 children aged between 5 and 8½ years were split into four groups according to their age. Each group was then divided into 3 subgroups: <br> a) The **standard group** — standard conservation task using counters. Two questions. <br> b) The **one judgement** task — only one question was asked, after the counters were moved. <br> c) The **fixed array control** — they only saw the display **after** it had been changed. |
| **Results:** | They found that younger children did better in the **one judgement** condition than the standard condition, but **older children** always did better overall. |
| **Conclusion:** | The study supports Samuel and Bryant's argument that two questions may confuse children. But, it still shows that conservation improves with age, so it doesn't disprove Piaget. |
| **Evaluation:** | This was a **laboratory experiment** so there was good **control** of the variables. However, lab experiments also lack **ecological validity** — the participants were not in a natural situation, so the results can't be **generalised** to real life. It's also possible that the results were affected by a third variable — e.g. younger children may have performed worse because they were more **intimidated** by the experimental situation. |

# Theories of Child Development

## Freud (1909) Talked About 'Psychosexual Development'

Freud claimed that a lot of our development is determined by unconscious forces — things in your mind that you're not aware of (see pages 76-77). The three main parts of the personality are the **id**, the **ego** and the **superego**:

1) The **id** is the basic animal part of the personality that contains our innate, aggressive and sexual instincts. It wants to be satisfied by whatever means possible, and obeys the **pleasure principle**.

2) The **ego** is the conscious, rational mind. It negotiates between the id and the superego to work out if you can have what you want — it works on the **reality principle**.

3) The **superego** is your conscience. It's the moral part of the personality and includes ideas about how to behave that were learnt from your parents.

The ego and the superego develop as the child goes through **five stages** of psychosexual development — the **oral**, **anal**, **phallic**, **latent**, and **genital** stages. Is anyone starting to think he was a bit nuts...?

**Comments on Freud's theory of development:**

1) Freud's theory places emphasis on how experiences in early childhood can affect later development. This has formed the basis for lots of other important theories.

2) Because they're based on the **unconscious mind**, Freud's theories are **unfalsifiable** (can't be **proved** wrong).

3) The theory is based on case studies of people in 'distress', so the findings can't be **generalised** to everyone else.

4) The unscientific research methods mean it's not possible to establish **cause and effect**.

### Freud (1909) — The case study of Little Hans

| | |
|---|---|
| **Method:** | Freud carried out a **case study** of a child called Hans who had a phobia of horses. Hans was observed by his father, who made notes of Hans's dreams and stuff he said, and then relayed his findings to Freud for analysis. |
| **Results:** | Hans was afraid of horses because he thought they might bite him or fall on him. During the study he developed an interest in his 'widdler'. His mum had told him not to play with it or she'd cut it off. Hans told his dad about a dream where he was married to his mum and his dad was now his grandfather. |
| **Conclusion:** | Freud's interpretation of these findings was that Hans had reached the **phallic stage** of development and showed evidence of the **Oedipus complex** — he wanted to have an exclusive relationship with his mother and was jealous of his father. Hans had sexual feelings for his mother, shown partly by his dream of marrying her. The horse symbolised Hans's father because, to him, they both had big penises. His fear of horses is an example of **displacement** — a **defence mechanism** that protected him from his real fear of his father. Hans suffered from **castration anxiety**. He was afraid that he would be castrated by his father if he found out about his feelings for his mother. This was symbolised by Hans's fear that a horse would bite him. |
| **Evaluation:** | This was a **case study**, meaning that it provided lots of detailed data about the subject. The findings provided evidence to support Freud's theories. However, the results were based entirely on observation and interpretation. This means they could have easily been caused by a third variable (e.g. Hans's castration anxiety might have come from his mother threatening to cut his penis off...). Also, before the study Hans had been frightened by a horse falling down in the street, which could explain his fear of them. Freud analysed information from Hans's father, so the results could be **biased**. As this was a study of one person, the results can't be **generalised**. |

OCR Core Study

## Practice Questions

Q1 Who suggested that children go through four major stages of cognitive development?

Q2 What is conservation?

Q3 What are Freud's five stages of psychosexual development?

**Exam Questions**

Q1 Outline Samuel and Bryant's (1984) method for the study of conservation. [6 marks]

Q2 Describe the research method used in Freud's (1909) study and give one limitation of it. [4 marks]

## Stages of development — crying, shouting, sulking, drinking...

*Personally, I think Freud was a nutter. A funny thing about him is that a lot of his ideas came from studying himself. You'd think he'd be a bit embarrassed to admit to all the mother-fancying and general obsession with genitals...*

# The Effects of Early Childhood Experience

*Behaviourists think that they can explain how children learn and develop by conditioning.*
*No, not by using a 2-in-1 to make their hair soft and sleek — a different type of conditioning. Read on...*

## The **Behaviourist** Approach to Development is Pretty Scientific

Behaviourism developed in early 1900s America and remained influential during most of the century.
It was pioneered by **John Watson** who proposed the three main assumptions that the approach is based on:

1) Virtually all behaviour is **learnt** from the environment. The only exceptions are inborn reflexes and instincts, e.g. the reflex to blink when you get dirt in your eye.

2) **Both humans** and **animals** learn behaviour using the same principles of learning.

3) For psychology to be **scientific** we should only study **observable behaviour** which can be analysed in quantitative terms, e.g. how many times a person does something. The 'mind' can't be seen or measured, so it can't be scientifically studied.

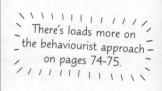
*There's loads more on the behaviourist approach on pages 74-75.*

Following these assumptions, behaviourists would usually do **experiments on animals** to study how they learn.
They'd then **generalise** these results to us **humans** to explain how we learn.

## Behaviourists Proposed **Two Types** of Conditioning:

### Classical Conditioning

In early 1900s Russia, **Ivan Pavlov** was studying how dogs' salivation helps them to digest food, when he noticed that they would sometimes salivate before they got food. Instead of just thinking they were hungry, he realised they had **associated** food with another stimulus, such as the sound of the door opening. He later made the dogs associate food with bells, lights and other abstract stimuli. This process of learning can be applied to human development:

*Pavlov's dogs got pretty hungry waiting for the food to arrive.*

1) Having needs dealt with and gaining comfort naturally makes a baby happy — it hasn't **learnt** to be happy, it's an **inborn reflex**.

2) So, comfort is an **unconditioned stimulus (UCS)** that produces happiness — an **unconditioned response (UCR)**.

3) The baby's mother will talk to it while she feeds it and changes its nappy, etc. So, the baby hears its mother's voice every time it's made comfortable and happy.

4) The sound of its mother's voice is paired with having needs met and being comfortable (UCS), so the mother's voice becomes the **conditioned stimulus (CS)**.

5) Eventually the sound of the mother's voice alone will make the baby feel happy, even when it isn't paired with having its needs met. The **CS** (voice) now causes a **conditioned response (CR)** — the baby has **learnt** to be pleased at the sound of its mother's voice.

### Operant Conditioning

Classical conditioning only applies to reflexive responses. **B.F. Skinner** studied how animals can learn from the **consequences of their actions**. Consequences can be classified as follows:

1) **Positive reinforcement.** This is when something 'desirable' is obtained in response to doing something e.g. after murmuring, the baby gets attention (the positive reinforcer). The baby is likely to murmur again.

2) **Negative reinforcement.** This is when something 'undesirable' (the negative reinforcer) is removed when something happens, e.g. after crying, a dirty nappy is removed. The child is likely to cry the next time the nappy is filled with digested baby food.

3) **Punishment.** This is when something 'undesirable' (the 'punisher') is received after doing something, e.g. after picking up something dangerous, the child is shouted at. The child is less likely to do it again.

There's a lot of evidence to show that animals and humans can learn by conditioning (see pages 74-75) but conditioning can't explain all human behaviour. We also learn by observation, as shown by **social learning theory**.

# The Effects of Early Childhood Experience

## Social Learning Theory (SLT) Accepts that Cognitive Processes are Important

SLT developed in the 1950s. It agrees with behaviourism that people can learn by conditioning but also claims that they learn a lot by **observation** and **imitation** of role models. This involves **cognitive processes**. People must focus their **attention** on the role model, **perceive** what they do and **remember** it in order to learn how to do it too.

A study by Bandura shows how children imitate adult role models.

### Bandura et al (1961) — imitation of aggressive models

| | |
|---|---|
| **Method:** | 36 girls and 36 boys with a mean age of 52 months took part in the study. The study had a **matched participants design** (children were matched on ratings of aggressive behaviour shown at their nursery school) and had **three conditions**. In the first condition, children observed **aggressive adult models** playing with a Bobo doll — e.g. hitting it with a mallet. In the second, children observed **non-aggressive models** playing with other toys and ignoring the Bobo doll. The third condition was a **control condition** in which children had no exposure to the models. The children's behaviour was then observed for 20 minutes in a room containing aggressive toys (e.g. a Bobo doll, a mallet) and non-aggressive toys (e.g. a tea set, crayons). |
| **Results:** | Children exposed to aggressive models imitated a lot of their aggressive behaviour. Children in the non-aggressive and control conditions showed barely any aggressive behaviour. Aggressive behaviour was slightly higher in the control condition than in the non-aggressive condition. |
| **Conclusion:** | Aggressive behaviour is learned through **imitation** of others behaving aggressively. |
| **Evaluation:** | This study provides evidence for **social learning theory**. There was **strict control** of the variables, meaning that the results are likely to be **reliable** and the study can be **replicated**. However, it has **low ecological validity** because the participants weren't in a natural situation. It's also difficult to **generalise** the results because a limited sample was studied — the children were all from the same school. The study encouraged aggression in children — this could be an **ethical problem**. |

## Some Comments on SLT, Behaviourism and Bandura's Research:

1) Bandura's study shows that **reinforcement is not needed for learning**. We can learn just by **observing**. However, the reinforcement the model is seen to receive may have an effect — for example, if you see a model punished for an action, you're unlikely to copy it.

2) Bobo dolls are designed for 'aggressive' play — you're **supposed** to hit them. As well as this, the children were shown how to play with the doll, so this study might actually be a test of **obedience** (see page 54) rather than observational learning.

3) Behaviourism and SLT emphasise learning as the cause of behaviour and so are on the 'nurture' side of the **nature-nurture debate**. This has implications for society. For example, children may imitate aggression from media role models. However, potential **genetic influences** are not taken into account.

## Practice Questions

Q1 What are the main assumptions of the behaviourist approach?

Q2 What is the difference between negative reinforcement and punishment?

Q3 Identify the dependent and independent variables in Bandura's study.

**Exam Questions**

Q1 Describe one similarity and one difference between Bandura's (1961) study and any other study in the developmental approach. [6 marks]

Q2 Evaluate Bandura's (1961) study of observational learning. [6 marks]

## Walk away from the Bobo doll with your mallet in the air...

*These psychologists are an interesting lot. Pavlov rang a bell over and over again to get a dog to dribble and Bandura and his gang beat up toys in front of children — whatever floats your boat I guess. Anyway, what you need to do is remember what they did — and more importantly what conclusions they drew from their results.*

# The Physiological Approach

*The physiological approach is all about looking at how physical, squidgy bits cause behaviour and determine experience. Yep, there's a shed-load of biology coming up...*

## There Are Three Basic **Assumptions** of the Physiological Approach

1) Human behaviour can be explained by looking at biological stuff such as **hormones**, **genetics**, **evolution** and the **nervous system**.

2) In theory, if we can explain all behaviour using **biological causes**, unwanted behaviour could be **modified** or **removed** using **biological treatments** such as medication for mental illness.

3) Experimental research conducted using **animals** can inform us about human behaviour and biological influences, because we share a lot of biological similarities.

## **Genetics** Is Used to Explain Behaviour

First of all, here's a speedy recap of the basic genetic knowledge that'll be handy in this section:

1) At conception, the egg and sperm join up to give a total of **46 chromosomes**.

2) Each chromosome is made up of a coil of **DNA**, which in turn is made up of loads and loads of **genes**.

3) The genes contain the information that make us **unique** in appearance (e.g. hair, skin and eye colour).

**Darwin's theory of evolution** suggests that over time, individuals who are **better adapted** to their environment through having **better genes** are more likely to survive to reproduce and pass on their useful genes. Those who are **less well-adapted** will be less likely to survive to reproduce and pass on their genes. Eventually, their less useful genes will be eliminated from the gene pool for that species. Through this process of **natural selection**, early humans **became better adapted** to their environments.

Physiological psychologists reckon that **genetics** can explain "**psychological traits**". These are things like gender behaviour (things that men and women do differently), intelligence, personality and sexual orientation. They also study genetics to see which genes make some people more likely to develop things like mental illness or addictions. **Twin studies** and **adoption studies** are useful for investigating these areas (see page 42).

## The **Nervous System** Controls What We Do and How We Do It

Biology recap time again — this time for the nervous system. Just when you thought the fun was all over...

1) The nervous system allows parts of the body to **communicate** with each other.

2) The **central nervous system** (CNS) consists of the **brain** and the **spinal cord**.

3) The **peripheral nervous system** (PNS) is all the **nerves** connecting the CNS with the rest of the body.

4) In the body, **neurones** are organised into nerves — spinal and cranial nerves.

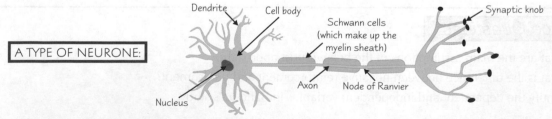

A TYPE OF NEURONE:

5) The **cell body** has **dendrites** that receive information from other neurones.

6) This info passes along the **axon** in the form of an **electrical wave** that ends up at a **synaptic knob**.

7) There's a small gap before the next neurone called a **synapse**.

8) **Neurotransmitters** are chemicals that are released from the synaptic knob. They pass across the synapse, to pass on the signal to the dendrites of the next neurone.

Physiological psychologists spend loads of time working out what different neurotransmitters do and how they can be influenced by things like **diet**, **exercise** and **drugs**. They also work out how to manipulate neurotransmitters with **medications**, to control different behaviours. For example, if a medication or diet was developed to reduce the neurotransmitters that signal stress, this could help people who get stressed out too easily.

# The Physiological Approach

## Brain Scanning is Used to Investigate Possible Abnormalities

There are various types of brain scanning out there — some just look at the **structure** and others look at **function**.

### 1) Magnetic Resonance Imaging (MRI)

MRI scans use **magnetic fields** to produce a **detailed image** of the brain that can show up abnormalities such as tumours and structural problems. It can also show **brain activity** by monitoring **blood flow** to different areas.

### 2) Positron Emission Tomography (PET)

PET scans measure **brain activity** using sensors placed on the head, which track a radioactive substance that has been injected into the person. PET scans can show which areas of the brain are more **active** when the person performs an activity such as counting. This helps us to understand about **function** and **communication** within the brain.

Both techniques are pretty **expensive** to use during research. However, it's useful to be able to see which parts of the brain are activated during certain activities, as different **functions** are performed in different parts of the brain. Certain functions, such as speech, problem solving and language processing, are generally localised more in one of the two **hemispheres** of the brain. This is known as **brain lateralisation**.

## The Physiological Approach Has Strengths and Weaknesses

### Strengths:

1) The approach can provide **evidence** to support or disprove a theory — it's a very **scientific** approach.
2) If a biological cause can be found for mental health problems or for unwanted behaviour such as aggression, then **biological treatments** can be developed to help individuals.

### Weaknesses:

1) The approach doesn't take into account the influence of people's **environment**, their **family**, **childhood experiences** or their **social situation**. Other approaches see these as being important factors in explaining behaviour.
2) Using a biological explanation for negative behaviour can lead to individuals or groups avoiding taking **personal** or **social responsibility** for their behaviour.

## Practice Questions

Q1 What is natural selection?
Q2 What does the CNS consist of?
Q3 What does PET stand for?
Q4 Why is the physiological approach described as being a very scientific approach?

### Exam Questions

Q1 Give two assumptions of the physiological approach. [4 marks]

Q2 Give one criticism of the physiological approach. [2 marks]

## MRI scans have shown that a student's brain patterns were identical when reading this page and when sleeping — coincidence...

*Actually I think this is pretty interesting stuff. I mean the way your brain works must be one of the biggest remaining mysteries in medical science — sure, they can start to recognise areas of the brain and stuff — but there's a long way to go.*

# The Physiological Approach

*Physiological psychologists aren't just happy with one research method. Pure greediness if you ask me...*

## There are **Two Main Ways** to Study **Genetic Influences**

### Twin Studies

1) Twin studies use **identical (monozygotic — MZ) twins** because they have **identical genes**.

2) They can be compared to see if there are any similarities in their **behaviour**.

3) For example, if both twins get very similar scores on an IQ test, that indicates a possible genetic cause for intelligence.

4) **Non-identical (dizygotic — DZ) twins** only share **half** their genes so it's less likely that their behaviour will be similar.

5) However, all twins are likely to have similar **environmental experiences** if they're raised in the same family.

### Adoption Studies

1) Adoption studies are used to compare family members with **close genetics** (ideally identical twins) who have been brought up in **different environments**.

2) Research into schizophrenia has found that adopted children are at a **higher risk** of developing the disorder if a **biological parent** had it, even if no-one in the adopted family has this type of mental disorder.

3) This indicates that the genetic influence is strong.

## Twin and Adoption Studies Have Some **Limitations**

1) MZ twins who are raised in the **same family** also share the **same environmental influences** so ideally MZ twins raised in different families should be used in research. Unfortunately though, there's not a massive number of people in these circumstances.

2) If there's a purely genetic reason for behaviour then in **all** sets of MZ twins where one twin has a certain behaviour, the other should also have it. However, research looking at areas such as mental health, intelligence and personality always finds MZ twins where this **isn't the case**. This means that there must also be factors other than genetics.

## *Gottesman and Shields* (1966) Investigated **Schizophrenia in Twins**

Gottesman and Shields found evidence to support a genetic cause for schizophrenia.

| | **Gottesman and Shields (1966) — schizophrenia in twins** |
|---|---|
| **Method:** | Hospital records for the past 16 years were examined to identify people with schizophrenia who had a **twin**. Around 40 sets of twins agreed to take part in the study, which was a **natural experiment** using **independent measures**. If it was uncertain whether a set were MZ or DZ twins, they were excluded from the study as a control of an extraneous variable. |
| **Results:** | The concordance rate (the amount of twins who both had schizophrenia) was about **48%** for **MZ** twins and about **17%** for **DZ** twins. The exact figures vary depending on the type of schizophrenia, but overall, MZ twins had a much higher concordance rate than DZ twins. |
| **Conclusion:** | DZ twins only share half of their genes and MZ twins share all of their genes. As the results for MZ twins are much higher, this suggests a **genetic cause** for schizophrenia. |
| **Evaluation:** | The results for MZ twins don't show 100% concordance, which means that there must be **other important factors** that influence schizophrenia. Although the researchers had a large amount of data covering a long period of time, it's unlikely the study could be **replicated** until new data existed. |

# The Physiological Approach

## Physiological Research Uses a Variety of **Research Methods**

### Experiments (also see page 6)

1) Experiments try to establish **cause and effect** by comparing groups and analysing any **differences** between them.
2) For example, the **Gottesman and Shields (1966)** study compared schizophrenia concordance rates in MZ and DZ twins.
3) Experiments are useful in this area because they can investigate possible **biological causes** of behaviour.
4) However, other **variables** have to be very tightly **controlled**, as they can affect the results of a study.

### Correlations (also pages 22-23)

1) Correlations describe the **relationship** between two variables.
2) For example, **Holmes and Rahe (1967)** found a positive correlation between the amount of **stressful life events** and **ill health** experienced.  As one variable increases, so does the other.
3) Correlations only show a relationship, **not** a cause and effect — e.g. we can't say that the stressful life events themselves caused the health problems.
4) They're useful for establishing relationships between variables and often lead to **further research**.

### Case Studies (also see page 7)

1) Case studies are used to investigate things that couldn't be investigated any other way.
2) For example, **Money (1972)** reported a case study of a boy who was raised as a girl after his penis was damaged during surgery.
3) Case studies are useful for investigating a situation in **great depth**.
4) However, they can't be **generalised** to other people as they're often unique situations.

### Questionnaires and Interviews (also see page 7)

1) Questionnaires and interviews are used to collect information from people **directly**.
2) For example, **Holmes and Rahe (1967)** used these techniques to get people to rate how stressful individual events were to them.
3) They rely on the **honesty** of the person but can provide **very detailed information**.

**Animals** are often used in physiological psychology experiments.

## Practice Questions

Q1 Do monozygotic twins have the same or different genes?

Q2 Which two techniques can be used to test for genetic influences?

Q3 Which of these methods was used by Gottesman and Shields (1966)?

**Exam Questions**

Q1 Outline methodologies used in the physiological approach. [4 marks]

Q2 Discuss the strengths and limitations of methodologies used in the physiological approach. [6 marks]

## Concordance — isn't that the name of a fancy old plane...

*Remember though, it's pretty rare to be able to say that something has a definite genetic cause.  Like with the Gottesman and Shields study, even if there's a strong case supporting a genetic influence, other factors always creep in — like environment and upbringing, or even what you had for tea last Thursday.  A lot more research still needs to be done.*

# Localisation of Function

*Yep, it's a page about brains. Interesting things. I mean, really, they're just a pile of gooey, squidgy, messy bits of meat. They probably taste quite nice, but how on earth can they see, think, feel, create consciousness, play chess...*

## Localisation of Function — Certain Bits of the Brain Do Certain Things

Certain areas of the brain are thought to be responsible for particular functions, e.g. vision, language, coordination... This is known as **localisation of function**.

The brain is split into two **hemispheres** (halves) — the right hemisphere and the left hemisphere.

**View from above**

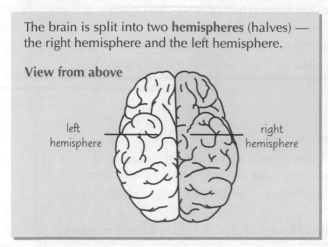

left hemisphere

right hemisphere

Within each hemisphere, there are four **lobes** — the **frontal** lobe, the **parietal** lobe, the **temporal** lobe and **occipital** lobe.

**Side view from left**

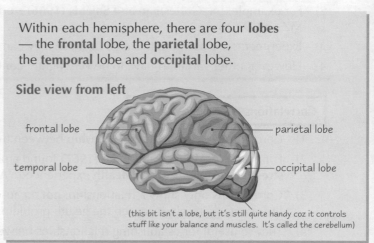

frontal lobe

parietal lobe

temporal lobe

occipital lobe

(this bit isn't a lobe, but it's still quite handy coz it controls stuff like your balance and muscles. It's called the cerebellum)

In most people, the **left** hemisphere handles the bulk of the **language** functions, **analysis and problem solving**, and **cognitive capacity**. The **right** hemisphere is more concerned with things like **spatial** comprehension, **emotions** and **face recognition**.

The **lobes** are named after their nearest **cranial** (skull) **bones** — each one is responsible for loads of specialised **functions** so they're generally not named after their function. (So, you wouldn't refer to, say, the memory lobe.)

## Split-Brain Surgery Provides more Evidence for the Localisation of Function

Since you haven't had a **biology recap** since page 40, it's about time for another...

Information from the right visual field (that's the right half of what you see) goes to the left hemisphere. Information from the left visual field goes to the right hemisphere (see the diagram below). Information passes through the **corpus callosum** to whichever side of the brain needs to deal with it.

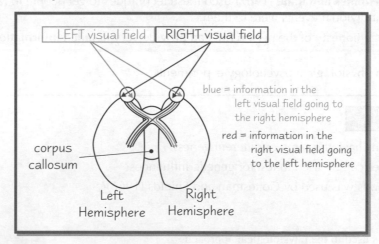

LEFT visual field    RIGHT visual field

blue = information in the left visual field going to the right hemisphere

red = information in the right visual field going to the left hemisphere

corpus callosum

Left Hemisphere

Right Hemisphere

**The effect of split-brain surgery:**

1) In very severe cases of **epilepsy**, the only treatment available is to sever the corpus callosum. This stops information and seizures spreading across the brain.

2) But a side effect of splitting the hemispheres is that information can no longer move between them.

3) Scientists have used split-brain surgery patients to study the different roles of the two hemispheres — take a look at Sperry's study on the next page.

# Localisation of Function

OCR Core Study

## Sperry (1968) Studied Split-Brain Patients

### Sperry (1968) studied individuals after split-brain surgery.

**Method:** The study involved a combination of **case studies** and **experiments**. The 11 participants had undergone split-brain surgery as a result of epilepsy that couldn't be controlled by medication. A control group was used who had no hemisphere disconnection. In one of the experiments, participants covered one eye and looked at a fixed point on a projection screen. Pictures were projected onto the **right** or **left** of the screen at high speeds so that there was no time for eye movement.

**Results:** If the picture was shown in the right visual field, all of the participants could say or write what it was without a problem. But if the image was flashed onto the left the split-brain participants couldn't say or write what they'd seen. They could select a corresponding object with their left hand, which represented what had been shown to their left eye (right hemisphere), even though they didn't know why they had selected this object.

**Conclusion:** This shows that different areas of the brain specialise in different functions. The left hemisphere (which receives visual information from the right visual field) can convert sight into spoken and written language. Usually information entering the right hemisphere can cross over to be processed in the left.
As the results show, this can't happen in split brains, so the information going to the right hemisphere can't be converted into language at all. But this doesn't mean that the right hemisphere is unaware.

**Comment:** Using case studies as well as experiments meant that Sperry obtained both **qualitative** and **quantitative** data. Also, using both method types meant that the **reliability** and the **validity** of the study were increased. However, the study only used 11 participants, which is a very **small sample** size for being able to generalise the results to others. But, it would have been difficult to find a large number of split-brain patients to study. Epilepsy is usually caused by **brain damage** and the patients had also been on **medication** which may have affected their brains. Therefore, it is hard to conclude that the ways they processed information would be the same as for people **without** epilepsy or split-brain treatment.
The study has also been criticised in terms of **ecological validity** — the experimental situation was artificial, so it's difficult to **generalise** the results to real-life situations.

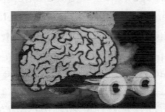

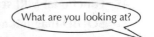
What are you looking at?

## Practice Questions

Q1 What is meant by 'localisation of function'?
Q2 Where does information from the right visual field go to?
Q3 What is split-brain surgery?

**Exam Questions**

Q1 In the study by Sperry:
a) Describe the sample used. [2 marks]
b) Discuss the limitations of the method. [6 marks]

## Brings a whole new perspective to being in two minds about things...

*I heard a story about a man who got attacked with a machete. Very nasty story — read no further if you're at all squeamish. Anyway, someone chopped right through the middle of his head with the machete. Blood everywhere, but the guy was absolutely fine. It'd gone right between the two hemispheres and not touched a single brain cell. Lucky man eh?*

# Brain Structure and Behaviour

*Physiological psychologists reckon that behaviour is determined by brain structure. Nowadays they use scanning techniques to look at people's brains and try to link structures and activity to various behaviours.*

## At First it was *Trickier* to *Investigate Brain Structure* and *Function*

Before brain scanning techniques were developed, psychologists relied on **case studies** of people who had experienced a **brain injury** or had **brain operations**. If the person had brain damage in a **specific area** and also a **change in behaviour** the assumption could be made that the two were related.

> For example, in 1848 **Phineas Gage** had damage to part of his **frontal lobe** after an explosion at work resulted in an iron bar going straight through his head (ouch). After the accident he was **less organised**, **more impulsive** and experienced personality changes including **increased aggression**. This led to the belief that this area of the brain is responsible for these behaviours. However, this is a case study of only one person, and so isn't **representative** of the population, which leads to problems with **generalising** the results.

But psychologists can't just sit around waiting for people with brain injuries to turn up so they can study them. For one thing, studies like that aren't conducted in **controlled** circumstances, so they're less **scientific**. And **ethically** we can't **deliberately** inflict this type of brain injury on humans. **Non-human animals** have been used to study brain structure and behaviour, but the differences between non-human animal brains and human brains mean that the results may not be that useful when we apply them to **human behaviour** (and there are still **ethics** to be considered when animals are used in research). So ideally psychologists could do with another way of studying brain structure and behaviour — ah-ha, that leads us nicely on to **brain scans**...

## *Brain Scans* Can Help Examine Patterns of Brain Activity and Anatomy

There are five basic techniques used:

1) **PET scans** (positron emission tomography — not what happens in the vets) show which parts of the brain are **active** during different tasks. By studying PET scans, we can link certain areas of the brain with particular **functions**. They also allow us to see where the brain is most active when we are **thinking** about certain things. They show average activity over a 60 second period, not moment by moment.

2) **CAT scans** detect **damaged** parts of the brain, tumours and blood clots. Brain **structure** is shown, not function.

3) **MRI scans** detect small tumours and provide **detailed** information about **structure**.

4) **Functional MRI scans** are **3D** scans providing **structural** and **functional** information.

5) **SQUID magnetometry** produces accurate images of brain **activity** by measuring the magnetic fields generated when neurones are activated. However, outside sources of magnetism can affect measurements.

## *There's Evidence from MRI Scans to Show Changes in Brain Structure*

OCR Core Study

### Maguire et al (2000) studied taxi drivers' brains

| | |
|---|---|
| **Method**: | In a **natural experiment**, MRI scans from 16 licensed male London taxi drivers were compared with a control group who had never driven taxis. All of the participants were in good general, neurological and psychiatric health, and had an average age of 44. All of the taxi drivers had been working for at least 18 months. |
| **Results**: | The average size of the right posterior hippocampus was **significantly larger** in the taxi driver group compared to the control group. Additionally, the increased size was relative to the length of time the taxi driver had been working — the **longer** they'd been working, the **larger** their right posterior hippocampus. |
| **Conclusion**: | The hippocampus is responsible for storing a spatial representation of the environment — it seems that the specific navigational demands on the taxi drivers have resulted in physical change. |
| **Evaluation**: | The findings of the study could be used to help those with brain injuries as it shows that the size of structures within the brain can be influenced through cognitive activity. This means **rehabilitation** could be tailored to the specific needs of individuals and their injuries. The study had a good level of **control** and could be **replicated**, which increases its **reliability**. The **sample size** is small though, and the results can only be **generalised** to male taxi drivers in London. Also, the results can't be generalised to **other areas** of the brain. |

# Brain Structure and Behaviour

## Brain Structure Has Been Investigated in *Several Areas* of Psychology

Psychologists have looked at **brain structure** as a way of **explaining behaviour** in many **research areas**. For example:

1) **Aggression** – Bard and Mountcastle (1948) found that lesioning areas of the brains of **cats** led to changes in levels of **aggression**. Their research suggests that the **hypothalamus** and **amygdala** are involved in aggression.

2) **Memory** – in a case study, Milner et al (1957) found that **HM** was unable to use his long-term memory effectively, suggesting that the **hippocampus** has an important role here (see page 27).

3) **Psychopathology** – Szeszko et al (1995) found differences in the **prefrontal cortex** when comparing people with and without **schizophrenia**, suggesting a relationship between them.

## Investigating *Brain Structure* to Understand *Behaviour* Raises *Debates*

**Reductionism (explaining behaviour using the most basic principles possible)**

1) The **negative aspect** of just using brain structure to explain behaviour is that it ignores other possible **biological** explanations for behaviour such as **genetics** and **biochemistry**. It also ignores **non-biological** explanations such as **cognition**, **social influences** and **learning experiences**.

2) The **positive aspect** of using brain structure alone to explain behaviour is that we can investigate very **specific** relationships to establish **cause** and **effect**. For example, knowing that a specific part of the brain has an important role in memory, aggression or mental health is useful for helping us to **treat** and **support** people after **brain injury**.

**Nature-nurture debate**

The nature-nurture debate is about whether behaviour is down to **biology** (nature) or **environmental influences** (nurture). Finding links between brain structure and behaviour adds to our knowledge of the **nature** side of the debate. This means that if a baby is born with a particular brain structure problem we now have a better understanding of how it will affect them in their everyday life. We should then be able to provide better **support**.

**Determinism**

Using brain structure to explain behaviour such as aggression and personality is **deterministic** because it suggests we have **no control** at all over these behaviours. This ignores our free will — our ability to make choices about how we behave.

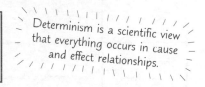
Determinism is a scientific view that everything occurs in cause and effect relationships.

## Practice Questions

Q1 What are PET scans used for?
Q2 Identify a practical application of the Maguire et al (2000) study.
Q3 Describe how investigating brain structure and function has an impact on the nature-nuture debate.

**Exam Questions**

Q1 For Maguire et al's study into taxi drivers:
   a) Briefly describe the method used. [2 marks]
   b) Suggest a change to the study and say why this would improve the results. [4 marks]

## Grrrrrrrrrrrrrrrrrrrrrrrrrrrrrrrrrrrrrrrrrrrrrrrrrrrrrrrrrrrrrrrrrrrrrrrrrrrrrrrrr...

*Well, what an interesting couple of pages. From a man with an iron bar through his head to slicing cat brains. It's not for the faint-hearted this psychology stuff, I can tell you. But it makes you wonder what you've got going on in that skull of yours. You might have the perfect hippocampus and hypothalamus to be an aggressive, schizophrenic, London taxi driver.*

# Sleep and Dreaming

*We've all got biological rhythms that affect our behaviour. They regulate things like eating and blood pressure, but the big daddy of body rhythms is the daily sleep/wake cycle. Read on to find out all about them — and try not to yawn.*

## The **Sleep/Wake Cycle** Takes Place **Once a Day**

Circadian rhythms are **biological rhythms** that take place **once a day**. The sleep/wake example is the most studied — we have a strong need for sleep each day. Several reasons have been put forward for the function of sleep:

**Evolutionary theory** says that sleep has **survival value**. For humans, it would have been an advantage to be still and quiet during the night to prevent being seen or eaten by predators with better night vision.

**Restoration theory** says that sleep allows the body to **restore** itself after a tiring day of biological processes. This explains why babies sleep much more than adults — they experience a big surge of development in a short space of time.

**Memory consolidation theory** says that sleep allows the brain to consolidate all the information it's absorbed during the day, and prevents any new information from **interfering** with this process.

*Sounds like too much thinking and not enough sleeping.*

## **Sleep** Can Be Split into Stages of Different **Brain Activity**

Electroencephalograms (EEGs) measure electrical activity in the brain, and are used to record the stages of sleep.

| | |
|---|---|
| Stage 1 | ~~~~~~~~~ |
| Stage 2 | ~~~~~~~~~ |
| Stage 3 | ~~~~~~~~~ |
| Stage 4 | ~~~~~~~~~ |
| REM Sleep (active sleep) | ~~~~~~~~~ |

1) Adults pass through the stages about five times a night, with each cycle lasting about 90 minutes. Who'd have thought we were so busy...

2) As you fall into deeper sleep from stages 1 to 4, the activity becomes **higher voltage** and **lower frequency**.

   **Stage 1** is a bit like deep relaxation, with lowered heart rate, muscle tension and temperature. It's quite easy to wake people up.

   **Stage 2** has slower and larger EEG waves, with some quick bursts of high frequency waves called **sleep spindles**.

   **Stage 3** has even larger, slower waves.

   **Stage 4** has the largest, slowest waves of all, because it's the deepest stage of sleep. Metabolic activity is pretty low in general, and the sleeper is very hard to wake.

3) After stage 4, the cycle reverses and goes back through stages 3 and 2. Then instead of stage 1, a period of '**active sleep**' occurs.

4) During the active stage, metabolic activity increases, and the body appears almost paralysed except for **rapid eye movement (REM)**. The EEG pattern is almost like when you're awake.

## Several **Methodologies** and **Techniques** are Used in Sleep Research

The following equipment and techniques are often used in **sleep laboratories**... Zzzzzzz... Hmmm, what..? Oh... yes. Variables, such as noise and distraction, are **controlled** to increase the **reliability** of the research. However, they're **artificial environments**, which may affect the participants' sleep patterns — reducing **validity**.

1) **Equipment** such as EEGs provide quantitative reports which can easily be compared to others. They have high reliability and changes in sleep stages can be easily identified. Other equipment used includes EOGs (electrooculograms) which measure the electrical activity of the eyes, and EMGs (electromyograms) which measure the electrical activity in muscles.

2) **Self reports** involve participants keeping a record of their dreams or estimating their length. They're useful for gaining information which couldn't be collected in any other way, but they're limited by the accuracy of recall.

3) **Observations** of patterns and directions of **eye movements** can be recorded and related to sleep stages.

# Sleep and Dreaming

OCR Core Study

## *Physiological Research Has Also Attempted to Understand* **Dreaming**

There are several theories about the function of dreaming:

1) **Winson (1993)** suggested that REM sleep evolved so humans could dream about important information that they needed for **survival** — for example, for hunting and hiding from predators. This information is integrated with **past experiences** and provides a **plan** for future behaviour. Today, we'd dream about current problems like money, jobs and relationships.

2) The **activation-synthesis model** by **Hobson and McCarley (1977)** suggests that **random neural activity** is muddled up with **existing knowledge** and memories, and expressed in the form of a **dream**. Hobson later suggested that dreaming is a **by-product** of the brain sorting out what to keep and forget. This explains why dreams are often about recent events.

3) **Webb and Cartwright (1978)** suggest dreams are used to **problem-solve** issues and help us deal with and resolve problems that have arisen during the day.

## *Dement and Kleitman* (1957) *Investigated* **Eye Movements** *During Dreams*

### Dement and Kleitman (1957) — eye movements during dreams

| | |
|---|---|
| **Method**: | 9 participants were monitored in a sleep laboratory. Their brain activity was recorded using an EEG. They were woken several times and asked to comment on the content and duration of any dreams. |
| **Results**: | It was seen that: <br>• Dreaming took place mostly during REM sleep. <br>• There was a positive correlation between the amount of time spent in REM and the person's estimate of how long they'd been dreaming. <br>• There was an association between the content of dreams and the pattern of eye movement. E.g. vertical eye movements when dreaming about looking up and down ladders. |
| **Conclusion**: | The findings suggest that there is a relationship between REM and dreaming. |
| **Evaluation**: | The study was designed to **control** for variables — amount of sleep, use of stimulants which could affect sleep, and the location of sleep. The **sample size** was small, making it difficult to **generalise** the results — they might only be applicable to this small group. In addition, these findings are not supported by later studies. The study lacks **ecological validity**, as sleep took place in a very artificial situation. |

## *Practice Questions*

Q1 What are EEGs used for?

Q2 Give two techniques used in sleep research.

Q3 What does the activation-synthesis model propose?

**Exam Questions**

Q1 For the study by Dement and Kleitman:

   a) Outline the results. [6 marks]

   b) Give one limitation of the methodology used. [2 marks]

## *Zzzzzzzzzzz... \*snort\* — Wha? Oh... yeah, sleeping... nice... Zzzzzzzzzz...*

*Last night I dreamt I was back at school, but school was also my house, and a bit like my old house and my new house, and my sister was there, then I can't remember what happened, but then we had some scampi but I don't know why cos I don't really like it. Then I woke up. Weird how your own dreams are always so much more interesting than other people's isn't it...*

# The Social Approach

*Social psychology is about how we influence each other.  Our behaviour is affected by the social situation we're in — so it might be normal to be naked in the bath, but it's not normal to be naked on the bus.  To be fair, not all of the research is about being naked, but at least it's got your attention...*

## Social Psychology Looks at How People Affect Each Other

1)  **Social behaviour** occurs when two or more people interact.  People interact differently depending on the situation — so you may act differently with a parent, a friend, a stranger, or when you're in a group.

2)  Social psychology also considers how we **think** about **other people**.  This is **social cognition**, which can involve things like **stereotyping** and **prejudice**.

3)  The influence of others can cause individuals to change their behaviour.  Social psychologists have studied why people **conform** (change their behaviour to fit in with a group), and why they **obey** authority figures.

## Social Psychologists Use Loads of Different Research Methods

Fortunately they're all methods that are used in some of the other approaches too.  There's more general stuff on research methods on pages 6-7.  And more on ethical issues on pages 16-17.

### Laboratory experiments

**Advantages**
- They're **highly controlled**, so the effect of the independent variable can be measured.
- This also means that it's possible to establish **cause and effect**, and to **replicate** the method.
- Participants in different conditions can act as comparisons.

**Disadvantages**
- They create an **artificial environment**, so studies have **low ecological validity** — most social interactions don't normally take place in labs.  Unless you're a rat.
- This means there are problems with **generalising** the results.

### Field experiments are conducted in **real-life settings** — e.g. hospitals (see Hofling et al's study on page 59).

**Advantages**
- The variables are still highly controlled, so it should be possible to establish **cause and effect**.
- Studies take place in the participants' natural environments, so they're more likely to capture natural social behaviour.  This means they have **higher ecological validity** than lab experiments.
- **Demand characteristics** are reduced if the participants don't know they're being studied.

**Disadvantages**
- It's very difficult to control all the variables in a natural environment, so the results can still be affected by **confounding variables**.
- Lots of field experiments involve using **deception** (e.g. Piliavin et al's study on page 62).  This has **ethical implications** — you can't get **informed consent**, and it can be difficult to **debrief** participants.

### Natural experiments look at **naturally occurring situations** — the independent variable isn't manipulated.

**Advantages**
- Studies take place in the participants' natural environments, and nothing is manipulated, so they're likely to capture natural social behaviour.  This means they have **high ecological validity**.
- Researchers can investigate variables that it would be **unethical** to manipulate.

**Disadvantages**
- Because none of the variables are controlled, experiments tend to have **low internal validity**. It's really hard to tell what actually caused the results.  This means it's difficult to establish **cause and effect**.
- Natural experiments often involve **deception**, which raises ethical issues.

# The Social Approach

**Naturalistic observation** is when the experimenter just **observes** behaviour, without manipulating any variables.

**Advantages**
- Participants are in a natural environment, and are often unaware they're being observed. This means that studies should have **high ecological validity**.
- Results from observations can be used to **develop theories**, which can then be tested in experiments.

**Disadvantages**
- Not controlling the independent variable means it's very difficult to establish **cause and effect**.
- The results are **subjective** — observers can be biased about what they record.
- Observation can involve **deception**, which brings up problems of gaining **informed consent** and **debriefing** participants. Ethically it's OK to observe people in places where they might expect to be observed by strangers — so you can watch them in the street, but you can't train a telescopic lens on their bedroom.

## *Surveys are used a lot*

Surveys can include **questionnaires** and **interviews**. They can be really useful, but the problem is that there's no way of knowing whether people are telling the truth. Unless you rig them up to a lie detector like on Jeremy Kyle.

**Questionnaires** can include **closed** or **open-ended questions**. Closed questions have a limited set of answers — e.g. yes or no. Open questions don't have a restricted set of answers — e.g. 'what do you think of Jeremy Kyle?' **Interviews** can be **structured** or **unstructured**. Structured interviews use pre-decided questions that are the same for all of the participants. In unstructured interviews the interviewers give the participant more freedom, although they might still guide the conversation to cover certain topics.

**Advantages**
- With questionnaires you can gather lots of data quickly and cheaply. This means you can have a large sample, making the results more reliable.
- Closed questions and structured interviews produce **quantitative data**, which is really easy to analyse.
- Open questions and unstructured interviews produce **qualitative data**, which is really detailed.

**Disadvantages**
- Questionnaires and interviews rely on self-reporting. This means people can lie in order to show themselves in a good light — **social desirability bias**.
- Interviews can be very time-consuming.
- It's easy to write bad questions. Researchers have to avoid **leading questions** (ones that lead the participants towards certain answers), or questions that can mean different things to different people.

## *Practice Questions*

Q1 What sorts of behaviour is social psychology concerned with?

Q2 Outline the experimental methods on these pages that involve manipulating the independent variable.

Q3 In terms of ethics, where can observational studies be conducted?

Q4 What's the difference between structured and unstructured interviews?

**Exam Questions**

Q1 a) Describe methodologies used by the social approach. [6 marks]

    b) Discuss the strengths and limitations of methodologies used by the social approach. [12 marks]

## Remember — social psychology is all about how people affect each other...

*Phew, it's all gone a bit research methodsy round here. Not sure how that happened. Still, it's good really cos this stuff turns up all over the shop, so learn it now and you'll be laughing all the way to the exam hall. I can just picture you now, having a whale of a time. Just remember to cool it to a gentle giggle once you're in there though, else you might get hiccups.*

# Types of Conformity

*Conformity* is when the behaviour of an individual or small group is ***influenced*** by a larger or dominant group.

## There's **More Than One Type** of **Conformity**

### Compliance

1) **Compliance** is where you go along with the majority, even if you don't share their views.

2) You do this just to appear '**normal**' — going against the majority might lead to exclusion or rejection from the group. This is called **normative social influence**.

### Internalisation

1) **Internalisation** is following along with the majority and **believing** in their views — you've accepted and **internalised** them so they're now your own too.

2) This might happen if you're in an unfamiliar situation, where you don't know what the 'correct' way to behave is. In this situation, you'd look to others for **information** about how to behave. This is called **informational social influence**.

## Asch (1951) Looked at **Normative Social Influence**

Asch designed an experiment to see whether people would conform to a majority's incorrect answer in an **unambiguous** task (one where the answer is obvious). Participants were asked to judge the length of a line in groups, but only one member of each group was actually a **real participant** — the others were 'in' on the experiment. The real participant always heard the others' answers before giving theirs. Participants **conformed to the majority** (gave the same wrong answer) 37% of the time (compared to only 0.7% of the time in control trials). Asch **concluded** that the participants were **conforming** to the majority through **normative influence**.

## Sherif (1935) Tested the Effects of **Informational Influence**

Sherif researched whether people are influenced by others when they're doing an **ambiguous task** (one where the answer isn't clear). Sherif used a visual illusion where a stationary spot of light appears to move. Participants had to estimate how far the light had moved. First, the participants made their estimates alone, then later they made estimates with two other people present. Finally, they were retested individually. When they were alone, participants developed their own stable estimates (**personal norms**), which varied widely between participants. Once the participants were in a group, the estimates tended to **converge** and become more alike. When the participants were then retested on their own, their estimates were more like the **group estimates** than their original guesses. Sherif **concluded** that they were **conforming** to the majority through **informational influence**.

## Zimbardo et al (1973) Studied **Conformity** to **Assigned Roles**

Zimbardo et al set up a mock prison to see if people would conform to the **assigned roles** of prisoner or guard.

### Zimbardo et al (1973) — Stanford Prison Experiment

| | |
|---|---|
| **Method:** | Male students were recruited to act as either guards or prisoners in a mock prison. They were randomly given the roles of prisoner or guard, and their behaviour was observed. The prisoners were 'arrested' at home, taken to 'prison' and given uniforms and numbers. The guards also wore uniforms and mirrored sunglasses. |
| **Results:** | Initially, the guards tried to assert their authority and the prisoners resisted by sticking together. The prisoners then became more passive and obedient, while the guards invented nastier punishments. The experiment was abandoned early because some prisoners became very distressed. |
| **Conclusion:** | Guards and prisoners adopted their social roles quickly. Zimbardo claims this shows that our **social role can influence our behaviour** — seemingly well-balanced men became unpleasant and aggressive in the role of guard. |
| **Evaluation:** | This was a **controlled observation**, so there was **good control** of variables. However, because it was an artificial environment, the results can't really be **generalised** to real-life situations. In terms of **ethics**, some participants found the experience very distressing. There's also a problem with **observer bias**, as Zimbardo ran the prison himself, and later admitted that he became too personally involved in the situation. This experiment doesn't take **individual differences** into account — not all of the participants behaved according to their new roles. |

# Types of Conformity

## Reicher and Haslam (2006) Developed the Ideas in Zimbardo's Study

1) In the **Holocaust** during World War Two, approximately 6 million Jews were horrifically murdered by the Nazis.

2) Psychologists had different theories about the soldiers who'd carried out the killings.
   Some thought they must be 'evil' individuals, but others thought they were 'normal' people who'd committed atrocities because of the social role they were in.

3) **Zimbardo's** (1973) study showed that normal people will shape their behaviour in order to fit into a social role, even if it's only been randomly assigned.

4) It seemed that the participants' behaviour was **situational** (due to the social situation they were in), rather than **dispositional** (due to their internal characteristics).

5) **Reicher and Haslam** (2006) recreated a similar situation to Zimbardo's experiment, but they were particularly interested to see how the group dynamics changed over time.

OCR Core Study

### Reicher and Haslam (2006) — the BBC Prison Study

**Method:** This was a **controlled observation** in a mock prison, which was filmed for television. The participants were 15 male volunteers who had responded to an advert. They were randomly assigned to 2 groups of 5 guards and 10 prisoners. They had daily tests to measure levels of depression, compliance with rules, and stress. The prisoners knew that one of them, chosen **at random**, would become a guard after 3 days. An independent **ethics committee** had the power to stop the experiment at any time in order to protect the participants.

**Results:** The guards failed to form a united group and identify with their role. They didn't always exercise their power and said they felt uncomfortable with the inequality of the situation. In the first 3 days, the prisoners tried to act in a way that would get them promoted to guard status. After one was promoted, they became a much **stronger group** because they knew there were no more chances of promotion. The unequal system collapsed due to the **unwillingness of the guards** and the **strength of the prisoner group**. On Day 6 the prisoners rebelled and the participants decided to live in a democracy, but this also collapsed due to tensions within the group. Some of the former prisoners then wanted to set up a stricter regime with them as leaders. The study was **abandoned** early on the advice of the ethics committee, as the participants showed signs of stress.

**Conclusion:** The participants didn't fit into their expected social roles, suggesting that these roles are **flexible**.

**Evaluation:** In contrast to Zimbardo's findings, Reicher and Haslam's prisoners were a strong group, and the guards were weak. However, it's possible that this was because Reicher and Haslam's guards were not as empowered as Zimbardo's, who were actively encouraged to maintain order. This study has been criticised for being made for TV — many people (including Zimbardo) argued that elements of it were staged and the participants played up to the cameras. Because this was an artificial situation, the results can't be **generalised** to real life. The **ethics** of this study were good — the participants were not **deceived**, so they were able to give **informed consent**. The participants were **protected** by the ethics committee and the study was abandoned as soon as they appeared to be becoming stressed. They were also **debriefed** and offered counselling afterwards.

## Practice Questions

Q1 What is normative social influence?

Q2 What's the difference between situational and dispositional behaviour?

Q3 Who were the participants in Reicher and Haslam's study?

**Exam Questions**

Q1 Describe how the social approach could explain conformity. [4 marks]

Q2 Discuss the strengths and limitations of the study by Reicher and Haslam. [8 marks]

## Oh doobee doo, I wanna be like you-oo-oo...

*Conformity's handy because it means you don't have to make any decisions for yourself... It's all about wanting to fit in with a group, even if you think it's actually a bit rubbish. Personally I reckon joining a group that involves being arrested and put in a fake prison isn't really ideal. I'd probably just say thanks but I'm washing my hair that week.*

SECTION FIVE — SOCIAL PSYCHOLOGY

# Obedience to Authority

*Obedience means acting in response to a direct order (usually from authority). It's mostly not a bad thing, and in some situations it's important — like getting out of the way if a police officer shouts "MOVE!". But it can also cause problems...*

## Milgram (1963) did a Famous Study of Obedience

### Milgram (1963) — the original 'remote learner' experiment

**Method:** Milgram conducted **laboratory experiments** to test factors thought to affect obedience. This 'remote learner' condition tested whether people would obey orders to shock someone in a separate room. It took place at the prestigious Yale University. **40 men** took part, responding to newspaper adverts seeking **volunteers** for a study on 'learning and memory'. They received payment for attending, which didn't depend on them proceeding with the experiment. The experimenter wore a grey technician's coat. Each participant was introduced to a **confederate** (acting like a participant, but who was really part of the experimental set-up). They drew lots to see who would act as 'teacher' and 'learner', but this was fixed so the participant was always the teacher. The participant witnessed the confederate being strapped into a chair and connected up to a shock generator in the next room. It didn't actually give electric shocks, but the participants thought it was real. The switches ranged from 15 volts (labelled 'Slight Shock') to 450 volts (labelled 'XXX'). The participant taught the learner word-pairs over an intercom. When the learner answered incorrectly, the participant had to administer an **increasing level of shock**. As the shocks increased, the learner started to scream and ask to be let out. After the 330 V shock, he made no further noise. If participants hesitated, the experimenter told them to continue. **Debriefing** included an interview, questionnaires and being reunited with the 'learner'.

**Results:** **26 participants (65%)** administered **450 V** and **none stopped before 300 V** (when the learner started protesting). Most showed obvious signs of stress during the experiment, like sweating, groaning and trembling.

**Conclusion:** **Ordinary people** will **obey orders** to hurt someone else, even if it means acting against their consciences.

## Milgram did lots of Variations on his Experiment

Ooh look, a table. That must say something good. Milgram carried out his experiment in loads of slightly different ways to investigate the effect that certain conditions would have on the results.

| Some of Milgram's variations on this experiment | Percentage administering 450 volts |
|---|---|
| Male participants | 65% |
| Female participants | 65% |
| Learner's protests can be heard | 62.5% |
| Experiment run in seedy offices | 48% |
| Learner in same room as participant | 40% |
| Authority (experimenter) in another room, communicating by phone | 23% |
| Other teachers (confederates) refuse to give shock | 10% |
| Other participant (a confederate) gives shock instead | 92.5% |

## Milgram's Experiment had Good and Bad Points

1) **Experimental (internal) validity:** It's possible that participants didn't really believe they were inflicting electric shocks — they were just going along with the **experimenter's expectations** (showing **demand characteristics**). But Milgram claimed participants' **stressed reactions** showed they believed the experiment was real.

2) **Ecological (external) validity:** Milgram's participants did a task that they were unlikely to encounter in real life (shocking someone). So the study **lacks ecological validity**. However, because it was a **laboratory experiment** there was good control of the variables, so it's possible to establish **cause and effect**.

3) **Ethical issues:** The participants were **deceived** as to the true nature of the study. This means they couldn't give **informed consent**. They weren't informed of their **right to withdraw** from the experiment. In fact, they were prompted to continue when they wanted to stop. The participants showed signs of stress during the experiment, so they weren't **protected**. However, they were extensively **debriefed** and 84% of them said they were pleased to have taken part. As well as this, at the time of the experiment there weren't any formal ethical guidelines in place, so technically Milgram didn't breach any. There's more general stuff on ethics on pages 16-17.

# Obedience to Authority

## Milgram Identified **Factors** that **Affected Obedience**

1) **Presence of allies**: When there were 3 teachers (1 participant and 2 confederates), the real participant was less likely to obey if the other two refused to obey. Having allies can make it easier to resist orders than when you're on your own.

2) **Proximity of the victim**: Milgram's results suggest an important factor was the **proximity (closeness)** of the **learner**. In the 'remote learner' condition, 65% gave the maximum shock. This dropped to 40% with the learner in the same room, and 30% when the participant had to put the learner's hand onto the shock plate. Proximity made the learner's suffering harder to ignore.

3) **Proximity of the authority**: When the authority figure gave prompts by phone from another room, obedience rates dropped to 23%. When the authority figure wasn't close by, orders were easier to resist.

## Milgram's **Agency Theory (1973)** Explains **Obedience**

1) When people behave on behalf of an **external authority** (do as they're told), they're said to be in an **agentic state**.

2) This means they act as someone's **agent**, rather than taking personal responsibility for their actions.

3) The opposite of this is behaving **autonomously** — not following orders.

4) Milgram claimed that there were some **binding factors** that might have kept his participants in the **agentic state**:

> **Reluctance** to **disrupt the experiment** — participants had already been paid, so may have felt **obliged** to continue.
>
> The **pressure** of the **surroundings** — the experiment took place in a prestigious university. This made the experimenter seem like a **legitimate authority**.
>
> The **insistence** of the **authority figure** — if participants hesitated they were told that they **had** to continue the experiment.

Before his study, Milgram believed that people were **autonomous** and could **choose** to resist authority. His **agency theory** shows Milgram's findings changed his mind about how much impact legitimate authority figures have.

> **Evaluation of Agency Theory**
>
> 1) There's lots of **experimental evidence** to support agency theory — Milgram's participants often claimed they wouldn't have gone as far by themselves, but they were just following orders.
>
> 2) Sometimes people **resist** the pressure to obey authority. This can be because of the situation, or because of individual differences (see page 57). Agency theory doesn't explain why some people are more likely to exhibit **independent behaviour** than others.

## Practice Questions

Q1 Outline the method of Milgram's (1963) experiment.

Q2 What is meant by 'proximity' and why is it a factor in obedience?

Q3 Outline Milgram's Agency Theory.

**Exam Questions**

Q1 From Milgram's study of obedience:
   a) What were the results of the 'remote learner' experiment? [2 marks]
   b) Outline why the validity of the study has been criticised. [4 marks]
   c) Outline two ethical problems of the study. [4 marks]

## *Pretty shocking results, don't you think?*

*You need to learn this stuff well in case Milgram crops up. You've got to admit it's pretty incredible that people would give someone a 450 V shock just because they were told to. Everyone always thinks that they wouldn't have done it if they were one of the participants, but really it's impossible to know. I definitely would have done though. I love electricity.*

# Obedience to Authority

There are different factors that make people more or less likely to obey authority...

## Milgram's Findings Tell Us About Why People Obey

### An Agentic State is When You Act for Someone Else

1) Milgram's **Agency Theory** (page 55) stated that when we feel we're acting out the wishes of another person (being their agent), we feel **less responsible** for our actions.

2) This effect is seen in Milgram's studies. Some participants were concerned for the **welfare** of the learner and asked who would take **responsibility** if he were harmed. When the experimenter (authority) took responsibility, often the participant would continue.

3) This **agentic state** was also in the experiment's set-up. The participants voluntarily entered a **social contract** (an obligation) with the experimenter to take part and follow the procedure of the study.

4) People can start off acting in an **autonomous** way (thinking for themselves), but then become obedient. This is known as an **agentic shift**. When Milgram's participants arrived for the experiment they were in an **autonomous state**, but as soon as they started following orders they underwent an **agentic shift**, and entered an **agentic state**.

### Gradual Commitment Can Make Us More Obedient

1) Gradual commitment means agreeing to something gradually — in **small steps**. It makes it **harder to refuse** the next request. In Milgram's study, participants were asked to deliver only a 15 volt shock at the start. This was gradually built up to very large shocks.

2) Participants might have been more **reluctant** to obey if they'd been asked to deliver the 450 volt shock at the start. They obeyed at the lower levels, so it was harder for them to justify disobeying the later requests.

3) Gradual commitment is also known as the '**foot-in-the-door**' effect. Once you've gone along with a minor request, the request could be gradually increased until you're doing something you might never have agreed to in the first place.

### We See Some People as Justified Authorities

Boris's authority may not have been justified, but he was the best damn cop in Düsseldorf.

1) We're socialised to recognise the authority of people like **parents**, **police officers**, **doctors**, **teachers** etc.

2) These kinds of people are **justified authorities** — they're given the **right** to **tell us what to do**. This means we're more likely to obey them.

3) When Milgram re-ran his study in some **run-down offices**, obedience rates were lower than when the study was run in the university.

4) He argued that the experimenter's authority was higher in the university situation because of the **status** of the university.

5) **Bickman (1974)** conducted a field experiment where researchers ordered passers-by to do something like pick up a bit of litter. They were dressed either in a guard's uniform, as a milkman, or just in smart clothes. People were much more likely to obey the person in a guard's uniform. This was because he seemed to be the most **legitimate authority figure**.

### Some Things Can Act as Buffers

1) **Buffers** are things that **protect us** — in this case **from the consequences of our actions**.

2) Milgram's participants were **more obedient** in conditions where they **could not see or hear** the victim receiving the shocks. When they were in the same room as the learner, there wasn't any buffer.

3) So... losing the buffer made it harder for Milgram's participants to act against their conscience and go along with someone's unjust orders to hurt the learner.

# Obedience to Authority

## Sometimes People Resist the Pressure to Obey Authority

### The Situation Can Make People More Resistant

1) More of Milgram's participants resisted orders if there were **other participants present** who refused to obey (see page 55). This suggests that people find it easier to stand up to authority if they have support from others, because they no longer have to take full responsibility for rebelling.

> **Gamson et al (1982)** found that support can help people resist authority, particularly if the request is unreasonable or unjust. They studied a **group** of participants **who felt they were being manipulated**. Participants rebelled against the unjust authority figure. This happened through a process of **minority influence** — with one or two people resisting the authority's requests at first. This rebellion then spread to the whole group.
>
> **Conclusion:** The presence of **allies** and **collective action** seemed to help the participants in their resistance.

2) This ties in with Asch's research on conformity. He found that participants were more likely to resist the pressure to conform if one of the confederates agreed with them. It seems that people are more likely to display independent behaviour if they've got support from others.

3) It doesn't really make sense to call this behaviour **independent**, seeing as it depends on having someone else there to agree with you... But just go with it...

### Resistance to Authority can be Explained by Individual Differences

1) If an individual has a high level of **moral reasoning** (thinking about right and wrong) they may be more able to resist an order that goes against their conscience.

2) One of Milgram's participants had experienced a Second World War concentration camp. She **refused** to administer any level of shock, because she didn't want to inflict pain on another person.

3) Those who resisted may have still felt personally responsible — they **weren't** in an **agentic state**.

> **Rotter (1966)** claimed that people could be categorised as having an **internal** or **external locus of control**. People with an **internal locus of control** take responsibility for their actions more than people with an **external locus of control**. This means that they're more likely to exhibit **independent behaviour** — they're less likely to conform, or be obedient, than people with an **external locus of control**.

> Sometimes people feel that they're being pushed too far or a rule restricts them too much. In this situation they might react by doing the **opposite** of what they're told. This is known as the **'boomerang effect'**.

## Practice Questions

Q1 Why might obedience rates have dropped when Milgram's study took place in run-down offices?

Q2 Give an example of a buffer that reduced obedience rates in one of Milgram's studies.

Q3 What did Gamson et al (1982) conclude from their research on independent behaviour?

Q4 How do individual differences influence independent behaviour?

**Exam Question**

Q1 What reasons have been given for why Milgram's participants obeyed in his study of obedience? [6 marks]

## I can never resist a man in uniform...

*The good thing about this obedience stuff is that it's mostly quite obvious. Everyone knows some people are more likely to obey authority than others. And the only explanation anyone can come up with for why this happens is that they just are, and that's that. So it shouldn't be too difficult to learn. And buffers is a pretty funny word too, which always helps...*

# Obedience to Authority

*You might have thought it was only Milgram who did obedience research... Oh, no, no, no. Once Milgram had done his study everyone wanted a piece of the action. And just a warning to you all, there are some naughty nurses coming up...*

## Cross-Cultural Studies *Tell Us About* Obedience *in Different* Societies

Milgram's research took place in the **USA**, so it only tells us about levels of obedience in that culture. Further research was needed in order to find out about obedience in other cultures.

### Meeus and Raaijmakers (1986)

| | |
|---|---|
| **Method:** | Meeus and Raaijmakers carried out their study in **The Netherlands**. They felt that Milgram's work lacked ecological validity, because people aren't often asked to give electric shocks to strangers in real life. So they wanted to test a more subtle form of obedience. They conducted a **laboratory experiment** with volunteers who had responded to an advert about research into stress and performance. Participants were asked to conduct interviews to test job applicants' reactions to stress. The job applicants were really trained confederates. The participants believed that if applicants failed the test, they wouldn't get the job and would remain unemployed. During the interview, the participants were prompted to deliver 15 '**stress remarks**' — criticisms of the job applicant. The remarks were designed to inflict increasing levels of psychological harm. The strongest remarks included telling the applicant, 'this job is too difficult for you'. The confederates acted confidently at first, but then broke down as the stress remarks were delivered, eventually begging the interviewer to stop. If the participants hesitated when asking the questions, they were prompted by the experimenter to continue. |
| **Results:** | Despite recognising the distress of the applicant, 22 of the 24 participants delivered all 15 stress remarks. |
| **Conclusion:** | A high percentage were prepared to inflict psychological harm in this realistic, face-to-face situation. |
| **Evaluation:** | **Ecological validity** was higher than in Milgram's research, because the interview is more of a real-life setting than being asked to give someone electric shocks. 96% of participants believed that the test situation was real, indicating that **experimental validity** was also high. **Ethical issues** include the use of **deception**. Because the participants were deceived they couldn't give **informed consent**. However, you could argue that this was scientifically justified — participants had to believe the setting was real for the experimenters to observe genuine behaviour. Another issue was **protection**, as the participants found the situation stressful. Another criticism of the study is that it's debatable how bad the participants really thought the 'stress remarks' were. There are loads of worse things to say than 'this job is too difficult for you'. How about 'you're ugly and your mum's fat' for starters? |

## We Can Draw Cross-Cultural Conclusions *from This* Research

1) Meeus and Raaijmakers' study was designed to improve on Milgram's study. It tested whether people would follow orders to inflict **psychological** harm, which is much more likely to happen in real life.

2) Their study was also very culturally relevant — The Netherlands was going through an unemployment crisis at the time, so job interviews were really important.

3) The fact that participants were still prepared to cause distress to people in a job interview suggests that obedience is a universal human characteristic. It provides extra evidence for Milgram's **agency theory** (page 55).

> However, there are **problems** with comparing these studies. The methods are different because Meeus and Raaijmakers wanted to improve on Milgram's study (and ethical guidelines meant they wouldn't have been allowed to replicate it anyway). But because the methods measure obedience in **different situations**, it's difficult to **generalise** the results and say that Dutch people are just as likely to be obedient as Americans. They were tested on different things, so we can't really know for sure.

> The other problem with comparing these studies is that they were done at **different times** (Milgram's was in the 1960s, Meeus and Raaijmakers' was in the 1980s). Societies can change a lot in 20 years — we can't know for sure whether Milgram's study would have got the same results in America in the 1980s. The results are **products** of **different times**, as well as different cultures. So trying to draw cross-cultural conclusions from them is a bit of a nightmare really.

# Obedience to Authority

## Hofling et al (1966) Studied Obedience Amongst Nurses

Hofling et al investigated whether nurses would obey a doctor if it meant breaking hospital rules:

### Hofling et al (1966) — obedience in nurses

| | |
|---|---|
| **Method:** | Hofling et al carried out a **field experiment** in hospitals in the USA. The participants were 22 staff nurses, who were phoned by a researcher posing as an unknown doctor. He instructed them to administer a drug to a patient before he arrived on the ward. He said he'd sign the paperwork when he got there. If the nurses obeyed they'd be breaking a number of rules, including: Taking instructions from a stranger, who might not be a doctor, Taking instructions over the phone without the necessary paperwork, Administering a drug at twice the maximum dose indicated on its label. |
| **Results:** | 21 out of the 22 nurses obeyed the doctor and prepared the medication. They said they were often given telephone instructions and doctors got annoyed if they refused. |
| **Conclusion:** | In this real-life setting, levels of obedience to authority were high. |
| **Evaluation:** | The nurses didn't know they were in an experiment, meaning the study has high **experimental validity**. Obeying doctors' requests is part of a nurse's normal role. This was a realistic position for the nurses to be in, so the study also has high **ecological validity**. The results provide support for Milgram's **agency theory** — the nurses acted on behalf of what they thought was a legitimate authority, so they didn't have a sense of personal responsibility for their actions. In terms of **ethics**, the study used **deception**, meaning that it wasn't possible to get **informed consent** from the participants. There is also the issue of **protection**, as the nurses may have been distressed when they were confronted with the fact that they were willing to break the rules. |

Well that was nice. Trouble is there's a whole big space left here that needs to be filled with something. How about some pictures of hospitals to remind you of Hofling...

Look at this nurse being all obedient like Hofling's nurses.

Look at this man being eaten by his mattress.

Look at these scary hands. Wooooh...

## Practice Questions

Q1 Outline the method of Meeus and Raaijmakers' (1986) study.

Q2 Why were Meeus and Raaijmakers' findings more ecologically valid that Milgram's?

Q3 Why are there problems with making cross-cultural comparisons between Milgram's study and Meeus and Raaijmakers' study?

Q4 How many of the nurses in Hofling et al's study obeyed the 'doctor'?

**Exam Question**

Q1 Describe one similarity and difference between Milgram's study and one other study in the social approach. [6 marks]

## Milgram was angry with the Dutch — he'd drawn a cross cultural conclusion

*It's a bit of a shame for old Meeus and Raaijmakers really, everyone remembers Milgram and ignores them. Never mind, lads — there's more to life than getting people to make job applicants cry anyway. You should take a leaf out of Hofling's book — invent a study about obedience in hospitals, then you'd get to spend your time giving orders to naughty nurses. Ooh saucy...*

# Research into Conformity and Obedience

These pages are just great. Look at all those lovely words just waiting to be read. This bit's about the implications of research into conformity and obedience for social change — basically, what we can learn from people like Milgram.

## Milgram's (1963) Findings Were **Revolutionary**

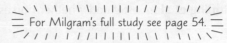

For Milgram's full study see page 54.

1) Before the study Milgram asked different experts on human behaviour (e.g. psychiatrists) to predict the results. They thought the maximum average shock that participants would go up to was 130 V, and that only someone with a **psychopathic personality disorder** would administer a 450 V shock.

2) He actually found that 65% of participants went up to 450 V, even when they clearly didn't want to.

Milgram's study completely changed what people thought about obedience, and it's had a huge impact ever since.

It showed that his participants **deferred responsibility** for their actions onto the authority figure. Milgram found the highest rate of obedience when the experiment took place in a university and he wore a lab coat. This exposed the huge amount of trust that people have in **justified authorities**. **Hofling et al (1966)** also showed this when they got nurses to break hospital rules because they thought they were following a doctor's orders.

### Application to real life

We often have no choice but to place our trust in experts, but with this comes the potential for abuse of power. A contemporary example of this is the case of **Harold Shipman** — a doctor who murdered patients by injecting them with huge overdoses. He was able to do this because his patients **trusted** him, and he got away with killing over 200 of them before anybody became suspicious.

## Zimbardo Looked at the Effect of **Deindividuation**

**Deindividuation** is when people lose their personal identity (stop feeling like **individuals**), and identify with a group.

1) **Zimbardo (1970)** replicated Milgram's experiment and examined the effect of different conditions.

2) He compared participants who wore their own clothes and were treated as individuals, to ones who wore **hoods** covering their faces and were spoken to as a group.

3) He found that the average level of electric shock **doubled** when the participants were wearing a hood.

When the participants were **deindividuated**, they became more **obedient** and more **antisocial**. Zimbardo later demonstrated this in the **Stanford Prison Experiment (1973)** (page 52). The prison guards wore **uniforms** and **sunglasses**, and they quickly became aggressive towards the prisoners. It seems that they stopped taking **personal responsibility** for their actions, and changed their behaviour to fit into their social role.

## Deindividuation Also Happens in **Large Crowds**

**Mann's (1981) study** looked at newspaper coverage of suicide attempts. It focused on the crowds that gathered below when someone was threatening to jump off a tall building or a bridge. The newspaper reports showed that people in large crowds were likely to start jeering and telling the person to jump. This was even more common when it was dark. Mann concluded that the **anonymity** you get in a big group can lead to more extreme behaviour, because the sense of personal responsibility is **shifted onto the group**.

### Application to real life

These studies help explain problems like police brutality and rioting behaviour. Zimbardo's research suggests there are ways of combating the negative effects of deindividuation — he found that when participants wore name tags instead of hoods, they gave less severe electric shocks. This has implications for social change — e.g. hoodies are banned in some public places. It could be that wearing hoodies makes people more likely to behave in an antisocial way. Or it could be that people find hoodies threatening because the people wearing them can't be identified. Or it could just be a load of rubbish.

# Research into Conformity and Obedience

## People in *Groups* Feel *Pressure* to *Conform*

1) **Sherif (1935)** and **Asch (1956)** (page 52) showed that participants' responses to tasks changed when they were in a group.

2) In Sherif's study this was because they were in an **unfamiliar situation**, so they looked to other people for information on how to behave. Asch's participants felt pressure from the group to give the wrong answer, just so they would **fit in**.

3) These findings have wider implications for society, as we rely on groups to make important decisions — e.g. governments and juries.

*Chris wasn't sure why the players had to be naked, but he wanted to fit in.*

> **Janis (1972)** found that groups having to make important decisions can be guilty of **Groupthink**. This happens especially in very **cohesive** groups, which are isolated from other influences, and have very **powerful leaders** — e.g. governments. Janis saw that members of the group converge their thinking so that it falls in line with what they imagine the general view of the group is. This leads to a unanimous decision that doesn't actually reflect what everyone in the group wants. It happens because individuals want to preserve the unity of the group. **Groupthink** is most common in situations where there's lots of **pressure** to make a quick, important decision.

Janis proposed ways of combating Groupthink:

> 1) Initially, group leaders shouldn't express their opinions, so other members won't feel **pressured** to agree with them.
>
> 2) One member should be given the role of **devil's advocate** (always expressing the opposite argument) to make sure that all possibilities are explored.
>
> 3) **Objective people** outside of the group should be consulted.

## Research into *Conformity* and *Obedience* has *Ethical Implications*

There are loads of ethical issues surrounding studies like Milgram's and Hofling's. The participants were deceived and put under stress. However, it's important with every study to do a **cost / benefit analysis** — consider whether the cost to the participants was worth the benefit of the findings to society.

> 1) Despite feeling pressured during the studies, a high proportion of Milgram's and Hofling's participants said they were **pleased to have taken part**. This was because they felt they'd learned valuable lessons about themselves.
>
> 2) Research into conformity and obedience can lead to **social change**. Studies like Milgram's **raised awareness** of the possible negative outcomes of blind obedience. Janis's ideas on **Groupthink** showed that some conflict within a group is necessary, not destructive. His ideas have been taken on board by group leaders to help ensure they make the best decisions.

## Practice Questions

Q1 What is deindividuation?

Q2 When is Groupthink most likely to occur?

**Exam Question**

Q1 Apply findings from the social approach to explain a real-life instance of conformity or obedience. [6 marks]

## Now all repeat after me — conformity is bad...

*The trouble with a lot of this research is that it forgets about all the good things that come from obedience and conformity. If you weren't so obedient and conformist then you wouldn't be sitting here revising right now, and that would be a crying shame. And anyway, a bit of good old-fashioned discipline never hurt anyone. Although a 450 volt shock might have done...*

# Situational Variables (Bystander Behaviour)

*These pages are all about how we behave as bystanders, especially when someone needs help. Whether we act to help them, or ignore what's happening, can depend on the situation we're in.*

## The Murder of **Kitty Genovese** Led to Research into **Bystander Behaviour**

**Kitty Genovese** was **murdered** outside her apartment block in 1964.

1) After the attack it was revealed that **38 people** had either seen or heard the attack, which lasted 35 minutes.
2) They reported hearing Kitty pleading for help, shouting that she had been stabbed and she was dying.
3) None of the witnesses called the police until 20 minutes after the attack.
4) Reasons given by the witnesses for not acting to help her included thinking it was a lovers' argument, being afraid, being tired, and not wanting to get involved.

The case prompted **Darley and Latané (1968)** to do a study into **bystander behaviour**. They felt that the witnesses might not have acted to help Kitty Genovese because there were **so many** of them:

> **Darley and Latané (1968)**
>
> Participants were told they were taking part in a discussion using intercoms with at least one other person, who was actually a confederate. They were all in separate rooms so that they couldn't see anyone. The confederate then starting making sounds like he was having a seizure and started begging for help.
>
> When participants believed they were the only person available, **85%** reported the problem within 2 minutes. When they thought they were in a six-person group, only **31%** did.
>
> This demonstrates a **diffusion of responsibility**. Although all participants considered the situation to be an emergency, they were less likely to help if there were more people involved who also didn't help.

## Piliavin et al (1969) Studied Bystander Behaviour

**OCR Core Study**

### Piliavin et al (1969) — bystander behaviour on the subway

| | |
|---|---|
| **Method:** | This was a **field experiment** to test bystander behaviour on a subway train. A man pretended to collapse on a train and the researchers observed to see if other passengers would help him. He was either white, black, drunk or carrying a cane in the different conditions of the study. |
| **Results:** | The participant with a **cane** was helped **95%** of the time. On average he was helped within **5 seconds** of collapsing. The participant who appeared **drunk** was helped **50%** of the time. The participant who was black and appeared drunk was less likely to receive help than any of the others. **90%** of 'first helpers' were male. The more passengers there were in the immediate vicinity of the victim, the more likely people were to help. |
| **Conclusion:** | Bystanders on subway trains are very likely to help others if they collapse, unless they appear to be drunk. Men are more likely to offer help than women. |
| **Evaluation:** | People were generally much more helpful than previous laboratory-based studies have shown. This study goes against Darley and Latané's findings for the diffusion of responsibility effect — passengers were actually **more likely** to help when there were more of them around. This was a **field experiment**, so it has good **ecological validity** as it took place in a **naturalistic** setting. This means it's possible to **generalise** the results. However, it also means that the results could have been caused by an **extraneous variable**, so it's difficult to establish **cause and effect**. There are **ethical problems** with this study — participants couldn't give **informed consent**, they might have experienced **stress**, and they weren't **debriefed**. |

# Situational Variables (Bystander Behaviour)

## Piliavin et al's Findings can be Explained Using Cost-Benefit Theory

After their study **Piliavin et al (1981)** developed cost-benefit theory. Well, not straight after. In fact it took them about ten years to get round to it. But whatever. You might also know it as the arousal-cost-reward theory or model. It proposes that we go through **three stages** when we're deciding whether or not to help someone:

| | |
|---|---|
| **1 Physiological Arousal**<br>Witnessing an emergency causes physiological arousal, like an increased heart rate.<br>Doing something to help can **reduce** this feeling. | **2 Labelling**<br>This is how we **interpret** the physiological arousal. We're more likely to help if we label the arousal as **personal distress** — helping will make us feel better. |

**3 Cost-Benefit Analysis**
We then weigh up the **pros** and **cons** of getting involved. **Costs** are things like putting yourself at risk, and the time it might take if you stop to help. **Benefits** are things like gaining social approval, and feeling good about yourself for helping. The **lower** the **costs** and the **higher** the **benefits**, the **more likely** you are to help.

This model can be used to explain the results of **Piliavin et al's (1969)** study.
Bystanders were much more likely to help the victim with the cane than the one who was drunk:

1) The **cost** of helping the drunk victim was higher than helping the one with a cane. His behaviour could have been unpredictable, so people could have felt they were putting themselves at risk by helping him.
2) The **benefits** of helping the drunk victim were lower. Bystanders could have felt that the drunk victim was partly responsible for what happened to him, so they felt less disapproval from other people for not helping.

Men were more likely to help than women:

1) The **cost** of helping may be higher for women than for men, in terms of putting themselves in personal danger.
2) The **benefit** for helping may be higher for men than for women — men might be expected to help more, and so feel more disapproval from others if they don't.

## Practice Questions

Q1 What was it about Kitty Genovese's murder that interested psychologists?

Q2 What were the findings of Darley and Latané's (1968) study into diffusion of responsibility?

Q3 What research method was used in Piliavin et al's (1969) study?

**Exam Questions**

Q1 From the study by Piliavin, Rodin and Piliavin:
   a) Describe the findings of the study. [4 marks]
   b) Outline why the study may be considered to have high validity. [2 marks]
   c) Briefly describe the cost-benefit theory suggested by Piliavin et al to explain the findings. [4 marks]

## It's no good looking away and assuming someone will learn this for you...

*Spare a thought for the people who made Piliavin's study possible — they spent weeks pretending to fall over on trains, just so you could have the pleasure of studying what happened to them. It might sound like fun for a couple of hours, but I reckon it would wear pretty thin after a while. Black / white / drunk man with/without cane, we salute you...*

# Contemporary Issues in Social Psychology

*Concepts from the social approach can be used to explain issues that are relevant to today's society. We've laid out a smorgasbord of contemporary issues for your delectation. It's definitely worth having a look at the studies on these pages — they can be really useful for backing up your answer in the exam.*

## Social Psychology Could Explain the **Abuse** at **Abu Ghraib**

1) In 2004 reports came out that American soldiers had been **abusing** Iraqi detainees in **Abu Ghraib** prison.
2) The guards took photos of each other posing and smiling while they tortured prisoners.
3) The American government condemned the guards' behaviour, and some of them were given prison sentences.
4) However, it was revealed that soldiers had been told to 'take the gloves off' when they interrogated prisoners. It seemed that they'd interpreted this as giving them absolute power to treat the prisoners however they wanted.

### Links to **Zimbardo's** Study

Zimbardo et al (1973) (page 52) conducted a study where people were randomly assigned the role of prisoner or guard. It was found that the guards started to act aggressively and cruelly, and the prisoners displayed 'learned helplessness'. These findings are mirrored in the real-life situation at Abu Ghraib. Like the American soldiers, Zimbardo's guards were given absolute power over the prisoners. It appears that they adapted their behaviour to fit into their social role. This was heightened by the fact that they wore uniforms, which deindividuate people, meaning that they feel less personal responsibility for their actions.

### Links to **Reicher and Haslam's** Study

Reicher and Haslam (2006) (page 53) carried out a prison experiment, but didn't explicitly tell the guards how much power they had over the prisoners. In their study the guards were much more reluctant to display their authority over the prisoners than in Zimbardo's. This suggests that the behaviour of the guards at Abu Ghraib can be explained by the fact that they felt they were given authority to treat the prisoners with unrestricted cruelty.

### Links to **Conformity** Studies

1) **Sherif's (1935)** study of **informational influence** (page 52) showed that people will look to each other for information on how to behave in an unfamiliar situation. One of the criticisms of the American army was that some of the soldiers were inexperienced. It could be that the guards at Abu Ghraib were following each other because they were unsure about how to behave.

2) **Asch's (1956)** study of **normative influence** (page 52) showed that people will **conform** towards a group norm so they don't stand out, even when they think what the group's doing is wrong. They could have been going along with everyone else because they didn't want to seem different.

No one was quite sure who started this silly walk behaviour.

3) These two types of conformity then lead to a situation where people feel even less individual responsibility, because they're just doing what everyone else is doing. This could be why the guards took photos of the abuse — in the environment they'd created, they began to think of it as normal and acceptable.

4) On the other hand, all Sherif and Asch's participants had to do was give an opinion about a spot of light or the length of a line. It's difficult to see how that's the same as torture. This means there are problems with **generalising** the results of these experiments to real life.

# Contemporary Issues in Social Psychology

## The Mi Lai Massacre is an Example of Obedience to Authority

1) In the **Vietnam War**, American troops fought guerrilla fighters called the **Viet Cong**. (A guerrilla army is an irregular armed force that fights a stronger force by small-scale raids and ambushes. The soldiers can sometimes be difficult to identify from civilians.)

2) After being told that there was a suspected Viet Cong presence in the village of **Mi Lai**, American soldiers attacked the village and killed hundreds of people, including many women and children, and even animals. But no weapons were ever found there.

3) Some of the soldiers seemed reluctant to carry out the attack, but still did. Later in court the lieutenant in charge of the unit said that he was just **following the orders** of his commanding officer.

Guerrilla fighters are not the same as gorilla fighters. Don't let this silly picture put you off.

In **Milgram's (1963)** study of **obedience** (page 54) 65% of participants obeyed orders to give someone electric shocks that they thought were extremely dangerous. Milgram explained these results with his **agency theory** (page 55). Just like Milgram's participants, the soldiers who carried out the Mi Lai massacre did something that they didn't necessarily think was right, because they'd been told to by an **authority figure**. They acted as **agents**, so they felt less individual responsibility for their actions.

A brutal bunch.

**Zimbardo (1973)** (page 52) found that when 'well-balanced' people were given the role of prison guards, and a uniform, they behaved brutally. He concluded that this was because they were fitting into the role they'd been given. It suggests that the soldiers who carried out the Mi Lai massacre were responding to the **role** and **situation** they were in, rather than being inherently violent or 'evil' individuals.

## Practice Questions

Q1 What happened at Abu Ghraib?
Q2 What is the effect of wearing a uniform?
Q3 How do Zimbardo's findings explain brutality?
Q4 How can the idea of informational influence be applied to Abu Ghraib?
Q5 How do Milgram's findings explain the Mi Lai massacre?

**Exam Question**

Q1 Discuss examples of how findings from studies in social psychology can be used to explain key issues in the real world.

[12 marks]

## So the moral of the story — don't trust people in uniforms...

*Not a particularly nice section to end on, but that's the social approach done anyway. Just remember the whole point of the social stuff is that it's about people doing things because they're influenced by those around them, even if that ultimately means doing something wrong. Well, I guess it's time for you to move on to pastures new — fly, my pretties, fly...*

# The Individual Differences Approach

*This section's all about individual differences — basically the fact that everyone is different. And an individual. Mind-blowing stuff. But what psychologists are really interested in is how everyone is different, and why...*

## Individuals **Differ** in Their Psychological Characteristics

The **individual differences approach** studies how psychological characteristics, like aggression and memory span, differ from person to person.

Psychologists argued for ages about whether an individual's personality is influenced by **nature** (inherited factors) or **nurture** (environmental factors). This is known as the **nature-nurture debate**. It's now thought most likely that **both** have an effect and interact with one another, so there shouldn't be much more debate over which one is solely to blame.

## There are Lots of Different **Perspectives** Within the Approach

These will be covered in more detail further on in the section, but for now, here's a brief overview...

### The Physiological Approach (see pages 70-71)

This approach explains behaviour in terms of **physiological** or **genetic** factors. It focuses on physical treatments for psychological disorders, e.g. using **drugs** or **electroconvulsive therapy**.

### The Cognitive Approach (see pages 72-73)

The cognitive approach is all about explaining behaviour by looking at an individual's **thought processes**. This approach puts abnormality down to **irrational and negative thoughts**.

### The Behavioural Approach (see pages 74-75)

The behavioural approach claims that all behaviour, including abnormal behaviour, is **learned**. It's believed that old behaviours can be 'unlearned' — treatment of abnormal behaviour is based on this.

### The Psychodynamic Approach (see pages 76-77)

The psychodynamic approach puts abnormal behaviour down to underlying **psychological problems**, often caused by past events and experiences. Treatment comes in the form of **psychoanalysis**, where the therapist tries to find and sort out these underlying problems.

## Several Different **Methods** are Used in the Individual Differences Approach

### 1)   Case Studies (see page 7 and 77)

In a **case study** you use **interviews** and **observation** to collect **information** about an individual or group. You can study behaviour over a **long period of time** — this means you could observe some behaviours that might not be seen in another type of study. Also, it's often possible to observe behaviour in a **natural setting**. However, in a natural setting it's harder to control all **variables**, and it's mighty tricky to **replicate** the study.

### 2)   Meta-analysis

This is where you analyse the results from loads of different studies and come up with some **general conclusions**. They're a good way of **bringing together data** (which is a general aim of the scientific process), and by doing this they reduce the problem of **sample size**. However, one problem is that they often include studies which may be **biased** or have **weaknesses** themselves.

### 3)   Correlational Studies (see page 7)

These use **statistics** to compare two **variables**. For instance, you might give a questionnaire to all participants to measure their stress levels on a scale. They'd then do another task, e.g. a memory test, for which they'd also get a score. A correlation would **compare** the scores to see if there is a **relationship** between stress and memory. But you couldn't use this to show that one **causes** the other.

### 4)   Physiological Studies

These include methods such as **brain scanning**, which can produce a detailed picture showing up any **structural abnormalities**. This means psychologists can make links between **structures** in the brain and **behavioural abnormalities**. However, scanning is a pretty **expensive process**, so it's not always possible.

# The Individual Differences Approach

OCR Core Study

## Psychologists Try to **Classify** People

The **DSM** is the American Psychiatric Association's Diagnostic and Statistical Manual of Mental Disorders. It contains all known mental health disorders, and offers a new **method of classification** — a **multiaxial classification**:

1) Individuals can be rated on **multiple axes/dimensions**. Diagnostic categories are used, for example organic mental disorders, personality disorders etc.

2) The DSM made diagnosis more **concrete and descriptive** than it had been.

3) Classifications are useful to acquire new information about a disorder. This can help in the development of new **treatments** and medication.

4) This type of classification has been criticised for **stigmatising** people and ignoring their 'uniqueness' by putting them in **artificial groups**.

### Rosenhan (1973) — psychiatric classification can be inaccurate.

| | |
|---|---|
| **Method 1:** | In a field study, eight 'normal' people tried to be admitted to 12 different psychiatric hospitals around the USA, with only one symptom — claiming they heard voices, saying 'empty', 'hollow' and 'thud'. |
| **Results 1:** | Seven were diagnosed with **schizophrenia** and all eight were **admitted** to psychiatric hospital. On admission, they said they were sane and had faked symptoms to get admitted, but this was seen as a symptom itself. It took, on average, 19 days before they were released, usually with a diagnosis of 'schizophrenia in remission'. Other, real patients could tell that these people were not mentally ill. |
| **Method 2:** | Rosenhan later told staff at a psychiatric hospital that one or more **pseudopatients** (normal people pretending to have schizophrenia) were trying to be admitted to the hospital. |
| **Results 2:** | No pseudopatients appeared, but 41 genuine patients were judged to be pseudopatients by staff. |
| **Conclusion:** | Medical staff could not distinguish the sane from the insane (although many of the real patients could). |
| **Evaluation:** | Being a field study, it wouldn't have been possible to control all variables, and so the results lose some of their **reliability**. Staff would probably not **expect** 'normal' people to try to gain admission to a psychiatric hospital, and so this might explain why the participants were initially admitted. 'Schizophrenia in remission' is a diagnosis that is **rarely** used, which suggests the psychiatrists concerned may not have believed they were really suffering from schizophrenia. There are **ethical** considerations in this study — people had their freedom taken away, mentally healthy people may have received treatments, professionals were deceived, and the study risked genuine patients not being treated. |

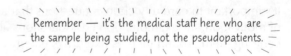
Remember — it's the medical staff here who are the sample being studied, not the pseudopatients.

## Practice Questions

Q1 What does the individual differences approach study?

Q2 List the four different perspectives within the individual differences approach.

Q3 What is meant by multiaxial classification?

**Exam Questions**

Q1 Rosenhan carried out a study to investigate psychiatric classification.
a) Outline the findings of the study. [4 marks]
b) Outline one way in which the study lacked reliability. [2 marks]
c) Identify two ethical problems associated with the study. [4 marks]

## *Get me out of here, I'm not crazy — I'm as sane as any other rabbit...*

*The first pages of a new section. Isn't it exciting... Anyway, before you get too excited and rush onto the next pages, make sure you've got to grips with the basics here first, and that you understand the Rosenhan study — it's an interesting one.*

# Psychometric Tests

*Psychometric tests are a method that psychologists use to measure individual differences. They're a bit like those tests you get in trashy magazines, but a **lot** more scientific. Right, enough waffle. Lets crack on — what star sign are you..?*

## Psychometric Tests *Measure Psychological Factors*

The idea with **psychometric tests** is that if things like personality or intelligence (psychological factors) exist, then we should be able to **measure** them. The **questions** are whether these things really do exist, and whether it's possible to measure them if they do.

**Traits** are aspects of personality — like punctuality, liveliness or laziness. Psychometric tests try to measure traits — the idea is that with enough information about specific traits, you can describe someone's **personality**.

### *Psychometric theorists developed standardised tests:*

1) Standardised tests provide information about how certain **groups** of people generally perform. The scores of an **individual** can then be compared to the scores of these groups. This is called... wait for it... wait for it... **standardisation**.

2) In these tests, everyone has the **same** set of instructions and the **same** task to do. This makes sure that differences in results are not due to differences in the test.

3) There are detailed **instructions** for administrators and people scoring the tests.

4) The tests, in theory, allow us to make **objective**, **statistically based judgements** on things like:

Clive had the capacity to behave in a normal way — he just didn't.

> a) people's **capacities** and **potentials** to act or behave in certain ways.
>
> b) the **severity** of psychological problems.
>
> c) the likelihood that someone will **cope** with a training course.
>
> d) someone's potential aptitude for certain types of **job**.

## Designing a Psychometric Test *Isn't Easy...*

...unless you're as great as me. When mere mortals are **designing** a psychometric test, there are plenty of things they have to think about:

1) It's important to carefully choose questions that are **relevant** to what you hope to measure. So in a test of motivation, for example, don't ask questions about bowls and dictionaries. Instead, think about centring them around themes like drive, energy and goals.

2) You've also got to think about:

> a) **scope** (who the test is for, e.g. children, adults or both)
>
> b) **accuracy** (how well the test measures the factor)
>
> c) **fairness** (whether everyone it's designed for will be able to use it equally easily)
>
> d) **practicality** (how easy it is to use, in general)

3) Sometimes the thing you want to measure will turn out to be made up of a number of **factors**, and so won't be so easy to measure. D'oh.

4) For example, **intelligence** may not be just a single trait, but be made up of variations such as problem solving, lateral thinking, social intelligence, spatial reasoning, memory, imagination and many others.

5) However, **correlations** exist between different types of intelligence. This suggests that although intelligence can be split up into different traits, they're not as independent as was first thought.

# Psychometric Tests

## Psychometric Tests Aren't Perfect

Never mind not perfect — often they're a bit shoddy. Learn why:

1) Tests are designed to measure what the person developing the test thinks they should measure.
   If there aren't **agreed definitions** of what is actually being measured, there can be difficulties.

2) There is also the difficulty of whether personality traits are **stable attributes**.
   It's difficult to know whether an individual will perform the same on a test on different days.

3) Many factors from age to ethnicity can affect test performance, so **fairness** should be considered carefully.

## Reliability and Validity are Important

**Reliability** and **validity** are pretty damn important in psychometric test design.
There's no point in using a test if it's not reliable and valid:

### Reliability

A **reliable** test is one that measures a trait **consistently**. To **test** reliability, you could give the same person the same test **twice** to see how the scores **correlate** (i.e. if they're the same).

When a test doesn't measure **consistently**, it could be because someone administered or scored it differently, for example.

Sometimes being the reliable one got too much for Jim.

### Validity

A **valid** test is one that really measures what it's **claimed** to measure. It's hard to say whether many psychometric tests are valid as there might be no agreed **definition** for the trait anyway.

## Practice Questions

Q1 What are psychometric tests designed to measure?
Q2 What is meant by standardisation?
Q3 What is reliability?
Q4 What is validity?

**Exam Questions**

Q1 Outline the limitations of psychometric tests. [6 marks]

Q2 Discuss the issues which need to be considered when constructing psychometric tests. [6 marks]

## The only thing this is testing is my patience...

*If psychology's going to keep claiming it's a science, I guess it needs to have some good, dry tests to keep all the geeks happy. None of them are perfect though, so you don't have to believe the results if you don't want to. Like if you take an IQ test and it turns out your score's the lowest out of everyone you know, it probably means there's something wrong with the test...*

# Physiology and Individual Differences

*Abnormality is a big area of research in individual differences. Some psychologists have tried to explain it using a physiological approach, but others have handled it with cognitive, psychodynamic and behavioural approaches.*

## The Physiological Model assumes Psychological Disorders are **Physical Illnesses**

The **physiological model** assumes that psychological disorders are **physical illnesses** with physical causes. In principle they're no different from physical illnesses like flu, except they have major psychological symptoms. When the same symptoms frequently occur together, they represent a reliable **syndrome** or **disorder**. The cause or '**aetiology**' may be one or more of the following:

1) **Genetics** — Faulty genes are known to cause some diseases that have psychological effects, e.g. Huntington's disease that leads to a deterioration of mental abilities.

2) **Neurotransmitters** (see page 40) — Too much or too little of a particular neurotransmitter may produce psychological disorders, e.g. an increased level of **dopamine** is linked to schizophrenia — **drugs** like cocaine, which increase dopamine levels, can lead to schizophrenia-like symptoms.

3) **Infection** — Disorders may be caused by infection. **General paresis** is a condition involving delusions and mood swings, leading to paralysis and death. It is caused by **syphilis**, and can now be treated.

4) **Brain injury** — Accidental brain damage may produce psychological disorders. E.g. in 1848 an explosion sent an iron rod through **Phineas Gage's** head, destroying parts of his frontal lobes. He survived, but he became more impulsive and disorganised, couldn't plan for the future and had a strangely different personality (see p.46).

## Research Has Been Done into the **Genetic Basis** of **Schizophrenia**

### Twin Studies

**Identical twins** share **100%** of their genes. So in theory, if schizophrenia has a purely **genetic basis**, if one twin suffers from schizophrenia then the other twin will too. **Non-identical twins** share **50%** of their genes, so the risk of both suffering should be lower.

| | Gottesman (1991) conducted a meta-analysis of twin studies |
|---|---|
| **Method:** | Gottesman carried out a meta-analysis of approximately 40 twin studies. |
| **Results:** | It was found that having an **identical twin** with schizophrenia gave you a **48%** chance of developing the condition. This reduced to **17%** in **non-identical twins**. |
| **Conclusion:** | Schizophrenia has a strong **genetic basis**. |
| **Evaluation:** | The meta-analysis was carried out on field studies, giving the research **high ecological validity**. Because identical twins share 100% of their genes, it might be expected that both twins would always suffer from the same conditions. The fact that both twins had developed schizophrenia in only about half of the cases means that **another factor** must also be involved. Identical twins tend to be treated more similarly than non-identical twins, and so the **family environment** might play a large role. |

### Adoption Studies

Adoption studies have also provided evidence for a **genetic basis** of schizophrenia.

| | Heston (1966) conducted an adoption study |
|---|---|
| **Method:** | 47 adopted children whose biological mothers had schizophrenia were studied. The control group consisted of 50 adopted children whose biological mothers didn't suffer from schizophrenia. The children were followed up as adults and were interviewed and given intelligence and personality tests. |
| **Results:** | Of the experimental group, 5 of the 47 became schizophrenic, compared to 0 in the control group. Another 4 of the experimental group were classified as borderline schizophrenic by the raters. |
| **Conclusion:** | The study supports the view that schizophrenia has a **genetic basis**. |
| **Evaluation:** | Interview data can be unreliable and affected by **social desirability bias**. However, interviews are a good way of getting data in a **naturalistic way**. The adopted children whose mothers didn't suffer from any conditions might have not shown any symptoms of schizophrenia **yet** — it can't be completely ruled out. |

# Physiology and Individual Differences

## Physiological Disorders Can Be **Treated** with Physiological Therapies

The physiological model says that once the physical cause of a psychological disorder has been identified, a physical (physiological) therapy is needed to treat the physical problem. One or more of the following may be used:

1) **Drugs** — Drugs can be used to change **neurotransmitter levels** in the brain. For example, **phenothiazines** reduce levels of dopamine and can therefore relieve symptoms of schizophrenia.

2) **Psychosurgery** — Psychosurgery is brain surgery involving destruction or separation of parts of the brain. **Moniz** developed the 'frontal lobotomy' in the 1930s to separate parts of the frontal lobes from the rest of the brain. This reduced aggression and generally made people more placid. However, it's **not a cure**, but a change — the **irreversible** changes to personality may have just made patients easier to manage. Psychosurgery is now only a last resort treatment for some disorders, e.g. very serious depression.

3) **Electroconvulsive therapy (ECT)** — During ECT, an electric shock of around 225 volts is given to a person's brain. This can help to relieve depression, but can also produce memory loss. Although quite commonly used in the past, it's now only used as a last resort therapy.

## The **Physiological Model** Has **Strengths** and **Weaknesses**

**Strengths:**

1) It has a **scientific** basis in biology and a lot of evidence shows that physiological causes **can** produce psychological symptoms.

2) It can be seen as **ethical** because people are **not blamed** for their disorders. They just have an illness.

3) Physiological **therapies** have helped relieve conditions (e.g. schizophrenia) that could not be treated very well previously.

**Weaknesses:**

1) Physiological therapies raise **ethical** concerns. Drugs can produce addiction and may only suppress symptoms rather than cure the disorder. The effects of psychosurgery are irreversible.

2) Psychological disorders may not be linked to any physical problem. **Psychological therapies** can be just as effective as physiological treatments, without any interference to physiological structures.

## Practice Questions

Q1 Give two possible causes of psychological disorders according to the physiological model.
Q2 What type of studies have been used to investigate the genetic basis of schizophrenia?
Q3 What is psychosurgery?
Q4 What is electroconvulsive therapy?
Q5 Give one strength and one weakness of the physiological model.

**Exam Questions**

Q1 Outline two assumptions of the physiological model relating to individual differences. [4 marks]

Q2 Give two limitations of the physiological approach to explaining individual differences. [6 marks]

## "Just chop up his brain and give it 225 V" — "Yes Dr. Frankenstein..."

So that's the physiological approach to abnormality. Make sure you know this thoroughly before you move on to the next page. And that means the key features, the studies, the treatments and the strengths and weaknesses. Phew. You don't want to start getting all the details mixed up with the other approaches. So, when you're ready, on to the cognitive approach...

# Cognitive Bias and Gambling

*Right, the cognitive approach to individual differences coming up. Psychologists have even looked into the thought processes that go on when people use fruit machines. Just an excuse to go to Las Vegas, I reckon...*

## The Cognitive Model of Abnormality Concentrates on *Thoughts* and *Beliefs*

The cognitive model assumes that behaviours are controlled by thoughts and beliefs. So, irrational thoughts and beliefs cause abnormal behaviours. Here's one version of the model that has been suggested:

> **Ellis (1962)** — The '**ABC model**' claims that disorders begin with an **activating event (A)** (e.g. a failed exam), leading to a **belief (B)** about why this happened. This may be rational (e.g. 'I didn't prepare well enough'), or irrational (e.g. 'I'm too stupid to pass exams'). The belief leads to a **consequence (C)**. Rational beliefs produce adaptive (appropriate) consequences (e.g. more revision). Irrational beliefs produce maladaptive (bad and inappropriate) consequences (e.g. getting depressed).

## Cognitive Biases *Distort Thinking*

> Cognitive biases are **mental errors** or **distortions of thinking** that lead to **perspectives** and **judgements** that can be very different to **reality**.

1) These faulty judgements can come about because we often subconsciously **simplify things** and use **rules of thumb** when processing information and making decisions.

2) Cognitive biases can be like **optical illusions**. Even when you're aware of the mistaken thinking, it still seems right. Because of this, they can be pretty difficult to overcome.

3) Cognitive biases appear all over the place. Things like **demand characteristics**, where people change their behaviour during a study because they think it'll please the researcher, are an example of cognitive bias.

## Single Pieces of Information *Can Make Us Change Our Minds*

One example of a cognitive bias is where you tend to take notice of a **single piece** of evidence even if it **goes against** statistically tested information.

1) For example, you might be thinking of buying a new car, and have a particular brand in mind.

2) The brand rates highly on tests of **reliability**, so you reckon it's a good choice.

3) However, one day, your friend who also drives this brand of car complains of a **breakdown**.

4) It's quite likely that you'll be inclined to go back on your decision.

5) It seems strange that we'd change our minds based on **one isolated incident** when we know of loads of **statistical information** proving otherwise, but it's pretty common.

*Yeah mate, great cars. Just one minor electrical fault. I'd highly recommend 'em.*

## Cognitive Biases Can Exist in *Gambling*

Cognitive biases also appear in **gambling**. People often believe that the **probability** of a future event, such as tossing a coin, is dependent on **past events**. When you stop and think about it, it seems quite daft, but you'd be surprised at how common it is.

> So, for example, if you're tossing a coin, and tails comes up four times in a row, you might expect heads to be more likely to come up next based on the fact that it's **about time** that it happened. However, as you probably know, this isn't the case. Each coin toss is an **independent event**, unaffected by the results of the previous tosses. Each time, heads and tails are equally likely.

# Cognitive Bias and Gambling

## Griffiths (1994) Investigated Cognitive Bias in Gambling

Griffiths compared regular gamblers with non-regular gamblers to see if there was any difference in the way that they make **judgements** and **perceive winning** whilst using fruit machines. Similar to the coin-tossing example, gambles on a fruit machine are all independent events.

### Griffiths (1994) looked at cognitive bias using fruit machines

**Method:** 30 participants who had previously only **occasionally** used a fruit machine volunteered to take part in a **field study** along with 30 **regular gamblers**. The study took place at an amusement arcade. Each participant was given £3, which initially gave them 30 gambles on the fruit machine. Participants were asked to try to stay on the machine for at least 60 gambles. If they reached 60, they were given the choice of keeping any winnings or carrying on gambling. Participants were randomly assigned to one of two groups — **'thinking aloud'** or **'non-thinking aloud'**. Thinking aloud required the participants to say all their thoughts out loud during the task. The time that each participant was on the machine was recorded, along with the total number of gambles, the amount of winnings and the outcome of every gamble.

**Results:** Regular gamblers made **more gambles** than non-regular gamblers, and were found to play **more gambles per minute**. There was no difference in **total winnings** but there was a difference in the **number of wins** — regular gamblers had more. Some regular gamblers **objected** to gambling on the fruit machine chosen for the study. Regular gamblers also made **more irrational verbalisations** than non-regular gamblers, such as personifying and talking to the machine whilst gambling (e.g. "the machine likes me").

**Conclusion:** Griffiths' study provided evidence for the existence of a cognitive bias in gambling. Regular gamblers played faster so it was likely that they would have more wins than a non-regular gambler. This means that they can **claim** to win more, even though it's likely that they also have a greater number of losses. This shows that an **illusion** is created, which causes the gambler to believe that they are doing well. The fact that some gamblers opposed to using the fruit machine selected for the study indicates that an **illusion of control** exists, where they believe that if they are familiar with a machine they will win more. Also, the fact that many regular gamblers **talked to the machine** shows that their behaviour was not in line with **reality**.

**Evaluation:** The experiment took place in a natural setting, increasing its **ecological validity**. However, this also means that the results could have been affected by **extraneous variables**. Only one of the regular gamblers was **female**, so the results may not have been **representative** of the whole population. Also, thinking aloud might have an effect on the **cognitive processes** taking place, making the study **invalid**.

## Practice Questions

Q1 What is cognitive bias?
Q2 What can cause cognitive bias?
Q3 Describe an example of cognitive bias.
Q4 Who studied cognitive bias in gambling using fruit machines?

**Exam Questions**

Q1 From the study by Griffiths:
a) Describe the sample used in the study. [2 marks]
b) Give one weakness of this sample. [2 marks]

## Fruit machines — the alternative to going to the grocer's...

*That can't have been such a bad study to take part in — being given money to play on fruit machines. Although I might've been tempted to just go and play on the grabber machine instead. Even though they always pack the toys in so tightly that nobody wins. I guess that's another cognitive bias — even though you know you won't win, you still have about ten goes.*

# The Behaviourist Approach

*As you'll remember from page 66, behaviourists believe that all our behaviours are learnt.*

## Behaviourism is Also Known as 'Learning Theory'

1) Behaviourism ('**Learning Theory**') started in America in the early 1900s, mainly through the ideas of **John Watson**.

2) Watson felt that earlier psychological research wasn't as scientific as it should be.

3) For example, Wilhelm Wundt tried to study consciousness using **introspection**. This involves analysing your own experiences. However, there's no way of finding out whether what a person said is true or not, so introspection can never be properly scientific.

4) Watson came up with some assumptions on which to base a **scientific** approach to psychology.

## There are Three Main Assumptions of Behaviourism

Remember — this is theory, not fact.

### 1) Nearly all behaviour is learnt.

The only exceptions are a few inborn **reflexes** (e.g. blinking when we get dirt in our eyes) and a few inborn **instincts** (e.g. instinctively running when in some types of danger).

However, evidence now shows that **genetics** can influence psychological features, e.g. genetics may contribute to the development of schizophrenia. Behaviourism still claims, though, that learning, and not genetics, is the cause of the **majority** of behaviours, even if some vague genetic causes can be found.

### 2) Animals and humans learn in the same ways.

Humans can do much more complex things than other animals, but the **principles** by which we learn are the **same**. So, we learn to drive a car through the same principles as a cat learns to use a cat-flap. This is based on the idea that we can form **stimulus-response associations** between stimuli and our actions. However, although we may both use conditioning, humans can be said to use other forms of learning as well, such as **social learning** (see page 39).

'All learnt through stimulus-response associations'. Pretty impressive, but does beg the question 'why?'

### 3) The 'mind' is irrelevant.

We can't directly observe and measure a person's thinking. So we can only obtain **testable scientific data** by studying behaviour.

However, although **cognitive abilities** cannot be directly, scientifically measured, they may give a more complete explanation of behaviour — as shown by **Social Learning Theory** (see page 39).

## Behaviourists Use Their Assumptions to Design Research Methods

The research methods used by the behaviourists follow directly from their **assumptions**, as follows:

**1 — Nearly all behaviour is learnt.**
So, understanding the principles of **learning** is the main research goal.

**2 — Animals and humans learn in the same ways.**
**Animals** can be used as research subjects because what is true for them should also be true for humans. Using animals has **practical advantages**, e.g. they are easy to keep, in many circumstances they don't know they are being studied and so behave 'naturally', and procedures can be used with them which would be illegal with humans (e.g. cutting out bits of their brains to see what happens).

**3 — The 'mind' is irrelevant.**
Behaviourists only observe **quantifiable behaviour** — e.g. how many times a lever is pressed, how long it takes to solve a puzzle. Typical research therefore involves **laboratory experiments** on animals, to see how they learn.

# The Behaviourist Approach

1) **Pavlov's research on classical conditioning.** Pavlov wasn't a behaviourist, but his work was useful to them. He showed how dogs could be '**conditioned**' to produce a reflexive response (e.g. salivation) to a stimulus that would not normally trigger that response (e.g. a bell). Pavlov **precisely measured** how much saliva his dogs produced and showed that it increased each time the bell was rung before feeding.

2) **Skinner's research on operant conditioning.** Hungry pigeons were placed in a box and fed once every 15 seconds. The pigeons began to show **unusual behaviours** such as walking in circles and stretching their neck just before being fed. Skinner reckoned that the pigeons had come to **associate** the strange behaviours with being fed — in other words, they believed that they had to walk in circles to get food.

3) **Human research.** Some experiments were done on humans, e.g. Watson and Rayner's experiment on '**Little Albert**':

| | **Watson and Rayner (1920) showed fear could be learned** |
|---|---|
| **Method:** | The participant was an 11-month-old boy called 'Little Albert'. He showed no fear of white fluffy objects such as rats or rabbits. The researchers tried to create a conditioned response to these objects. A white rat was placed in front of Little Albert. As he reached out for it, a metal bar was struck loudly behind his head. This was repeated twice at first, then 5 more times a week later. |
| **Results:** | When Little Albert was shown a rat, he would start to cry. This also extended to other white fluffy objects, such as a white Santa Claus beard. |
| **Conclusion:** | A fear response to white fluffy objects had been **conditioned** in Little Albert, showing that abnormal behaviour can be **learned**. |
| **Evaluation:** | The experiment was extremely **unethical** — such an experiment couldn't be repeated today. Also, **not everyone** goes on to develop a fear or phobia after a negative situation, so learning theory can't be the full story. |

Absolutely nothing to worry about, Mrs Albert — all within the guidelines.

**Comment** — Behaviourists are often criticised for focusing research on animals. Plenty of research has been done on humans, which has shown things like:
- our **genes** influence our behaviour
- we can **learn in ways other than conditioning**
- that **mental, cognitive processes are relevant** to understanding behaviour.

Q1 Who pioneered behaviourism?
Q2 What did behaviourists think about the mind?
Q3 Why may the assumptions of behaviourism be questioned?

**Exam Questions**

| | |
|---|---|
| Q1 Outline two assumptions of the behaviourist perspective. | [4 marks] |
| Q2 Outline one limitation of the behaviourist perspective. | [2 marks] |

## Learn like a dolphin — lob live fish in the air and catch them in your mouth...

*The behaviourist assumption is that humans and animals learn in the same way. Still, I've never met an animal who was scared of Santa. Apart from the reindeer of course, they can't stand him. But that's because there's no pension scheme — once those reindeer can't fly any more, that's it. He sends them off to the glue factory. And uses their antlers as shoe horns.*

# The Psychodynamic Approach

*Psychodynamic theories like to explain behaviour by talking about unconscious causes — talk about abnormal...*

## Freud Developed The **Psychodynamic** Approach

'**Psycho**' refers to the mind and '**dynamic**' refers to change or activity.
So, this approach emphasises the **active nature** of mental processes and their role in **shaping personality** and **behaviour**.
This approach was developed by **Sigmund Freud** (1856-1939), in the 18th/early 19th centuries.  It assumes that:

> 1) Human behaviour has **unconscious causes** that we're not aware of.
>
> 2) From birth, humans have a need to fulfil basic biological **motivations** — for food, sleep, warmth etc.
>
> 3) **Childhood experiences** are a really important influence on the development of adult personality and psychological disorders.

## Freud Said There Are Three **Levels of Consciousness**

Freud was interested in '**hysteria**', a disorder involving physical symptoms such as headaches, paralysis and blindness, but with no apparent physical cause.  As his patients couldn't give any **conscious** reasons, Freud concluded they had an **unconscious** mind and that's where the cause of the hysteria was.  He identified three levels of consciousness:

> 1) **Conscious**. This is what we are **aware** of at any given time, e.g. what we are seeing, hearing, smelling or thinking.
>
> 2) **Preconscious**. This is made up of **memories** that we can recall when we want to, e.g. we can recall our address, phone number, childhood memories or what we did at the weekend.
>
> 3) **Unconscious**. This is made up of memories, desires and fears which cause us extreme anxiety and have therefore been '**repressed**' or forced out of conscious awareness. However, the unconscious still influences behaviour.  For example, it causes 'Freudian slips' and influences the content of our dreams.  This part of our mind can be accessed with the help of a **psychoanalyst**, using the methods that Freud developed (see the next page).

## There Are Two **Instincts** That Motivate Our Behaviour

Freud claimed that from birth, two types of **instinct** motivate our behaviour.
The two instincts are in constant **conflict** with each other, and one may **dominate** in a person:

> 1) **The Life Instinct ('Eros').**  This is the need to fulfil basic biological needs, such as for warmth, food or sleep.  However, Freud also claimed that infants have the need for **sexual pleasure**, i.e. they obtain pleasure through **erogenous zones** — parts of the body that are sensitive to stimulation.  Although this does not involve mature sexual needs, Freud claimed that '**infantile sexuality**' is a major motivation as we progress through the stages of **psychosexual development** (see page 37).  The energy of the life instinct is called '**libido**'.
>
> 2) **The Death Instinct ('Thanatos').**  The death instinct involves the urge to be **aggressive** and **destructive** to others and/or ourselves.  This causes violence, war and suicide.

## Freud Reckoned **Early Experiences** Influence Development

1) Each stage of psychosexual development focuses on **obtaining pleasure** through that stage's erogenous zone.

2) How parents raise a child affects how much pleasure is obtained through that stage (e.g. how strict they are when potty training, and what type of role models they are).

3) If a child experiences a lot of **conflict** or **anxiety** during a stage of development it becomes '**fixated**' with that stage and will remain, to some extent, attached to that erogenous zone.

4) This experience is all **repressed into the unconscious**, but influences adult personality. Severe fixation could lead to a psychological **disorder**.

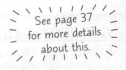

See page 37 for more details about this.

# The Psychodynamic Approach

## Clinical Interviews and Symbol Analysis Reveal Unconscious Problems

Freud did **case studies** on his patients using several **methods** to reveal the **conflicts**, **fears** and **desires** buried in their unconscious mind. These problems could then be faced, allowing the patient to understand and resolve them.

1) In a case study, a lot of **detailed information** about **unique cases** can be collected.

2) However, it's not usually possible to make **generalisations** from the results to the rest of the population.

3) Case studies often rely a lot on **retrospective data** (i.e. from the past) and so if this data is incorrectly recalled, the results become unreliable.

4) Case studies have some **ethical issues** in that some people believe that it's not right to **publish** detailed data about a particular person's problems. However, participants usually remain **anonymous**, are given a **different name**, or are simply referred to by their initials.

**Clinical interviews** and **symbol analysis** are the main methods of studying the unconscious mind:

### Clinical interviews
These are flexible, informal interviews. They may involve:

a) **Free association**. This is where the patient is given a cue and then asked to say whatever comes into their mind, however silly or embarrassing. By analysing what a person does and doesn't talk about, the psychoanalyst can identify unconscious influences, e.g. I say 'revision', and you say 'night out'.

b) **'Freudian slips'**. These occur when we do or say something that we consciously think are mistakes, but which really show our unconscious true feelings. An example given by Freud was how an MP once said, 'the honourable member from Hell', when he really meant 'from Hull'. How very rude. But you have to remember that this was before the Humber Bridge was built. Nowadays the MP would have to say, 'the honourable member from Hull, which does boast the sixth longest single-span suspension bridge in the world, so it's not all bad'.

### Analysis of symbols in dreams and culture
Freud believed that the unconscious can reveal itself in the form of symbols. They allow the unconscious fears, desires and conflicts to show themselves or be 'fulfilled'. However, we don't become consciously aware of them, and therefore don't feel anxious or guilty:

a) **Dream analysis**. Freud claimed that dreams involve **'disguised wish fulfilment'**. This means that we use them to 'play out' our repressed wishes — ones which would produce guilt or anxiety if we were consciously aware of them. The images we can recall are the **'manifest content'** (the superficial stuff), but the analyst can interpret the **'latent content'** — the true meaning.

b) **Culture**. Freud claimed that cultural art, theatre and literature are 'manifest content' which symbolically represents the 'latent content' of universal human needs and conflicts.

You should probably bear in mind that all of these methods depend on the **interpretations** of the analyst, so they're **subjective** and **not truly scientific**. Having said that, they still may be useful.

## Practice Questions

Q1 Explain the difference between the 'preconscious' and the 'unconscious'.

Q2 Why is early experience important, according to the psychodynamic approach?

Q3 What happens in 'free association'?

### Exam Questions

Q1 Outline one assumption of the psychodynamic approach. [2 marks]

Q2 Freud used case studies in his work. Discuss the strengths and limitations of using case studies. [6 marks]

## My favourite subject is (insert Freudian slip here)... Oops — I mean art...

*If you've ever called your teacher Mum, or boyfriend Dad, you probably just thought it was a simple mistake. According to psychodynamic theory, you're actually showing your deep-felt desires. Remember, it's not just what you say, but what you think about and what you dream that shows your unconscious mind peeking through — hands up who's scared now...*

# Multiple Personality Disorder

*This is a scary topic. Imagine if one day you woke up with no memory of the previous night, but everyone said you were acting like a different person... and you'd not had a drop to drink...*

## Multiple Personality Disorder (MPD) is Very Rare

1) **Multiple personality disorder**, or **dissociative identity disorder** (DID), is where a person develops different personalities.

2) These different personalities may have different memories, behaviours, attitudes and cognitive functioning, and may or may not be aware of each other.

3) There has been debate over whether such a condition actually **exists**. Having said that, people now generally believe that it does, and that it's a consequence of **extreme abuse** in childhood.

4) It's suggested that a **dissociation** (a lack of **connection**) from reality happens as a form of **mental escape** from trauma. This will produce changes in memory and perhaps, if this happens often, the person's whole sense of history and identity will change.

The **clinical characteristics** of MPD include:

1) The person is **unable to recall personal information** which would not normally be forgotten.

2) Two or more **distinct personalities** exist, each with their own perceptions of the environment and themselves.

3) These personalities take turns at **controlling** the behaviour of the person.

4) The disturbance is **not due** to other physiological effects, such as alcohol abuse or epilepsy.

## Eve White Was the First Convincing Account of MPD

Yeah, I know this looks bad, but it's actually quite interesting. Actually, I don't know why I'm hyping it up — you've got to learn it whether it's as dull as James Blunt and David Gray all rolled into one, or not.

### Thigpen and Cleckley (1954) — case study of Eve White

Eve White's real name was Christine Sizemore. She was a 25-year-old married woman, who after suffering from **headaches**, **blackouts** and **memory loss**, was referred to a psychiatrist.

Her psychiatrist received a letter with the final lines written in a different handwriting and tone. Eve White said she had started a letter but not finished it. In a therapy session, she asked if hearing voices was a sign of insanity. Then she put her hands to her head as if in pain — and another personality who called herself '**Eve Black**' appeared. Eve White was **not aware** of Eve Black until informed, but Eve Black was **aware** and critical of Eve White.

A number of Eve's **life events** suggested that she was suffering from **MPD**:
Eve White recalled being punished for things she didn't remember doing in childhood. Her parents confirmed this. Eve Black claimed responsibility for many childhood pranks. Additionally, Eve Black denied knowledge of Eve White's husband and of any relationship to her daughter. She claimed to have been married to someone else — a husband who Eve White claimed no knowledge of. A relative revealed that there had been a previous marriage, and later Eve Black admitted that this had been a time when she was in control, not Eve White.

**Psychometric tests** revealed the extent of the two personalities' differences: Eve White had a **slightly higher IQ** and **memory** function in tests. Eve White was found to be serious, anxious, conscientious and emotionally **repressed**. Eve Black, by comparison, was hedonistic, shallow, irresponsible and less anxious, lacked compassion and often **regressed** to childlike behaviour. Only Eve White could be hypnotised and was thought to be the **dominant** personality. 'Black' was Eve White's maiden name, which suggested that Eve Black was not a different personality as such, but the same personality at an earlier stage of life, perhaps brought about by a desire to return to this earlier, more irresponsible time of life.

During the progress of therapy, improvements seemed to occur. Eve White stopped having headaches and blackouts and hearing voices. Eve Black also caused less trouble, although still acted quite irresponsibly. Later, a third personality, **Jane**, appeared who was more mature, capable and interesting than Eve White, yet lacked Eve Black's faults. Jane was seen as a compromise between the two previous personalities. In the years after Thigpen and Cleckley's case study, over 20 different personalities appeared. The final one was **Christine Costner Sizemore** (her real name), who said she had **assimilated** her different selves.

*OCR Core Study*

# Multiple Personality Disorder

## There is Debate Over Whether Some MPD Cases are *Genuine*

1) At the time of Thigpen and Cleckley's case study, **very few** cases of MPD had been reported.

2) A rash of reported cases followed a popular book and film called **Sybil** about a case of MPD.

3) It has been suggested that this book and film led to an inadvertent trend among therapists to **diagnose** their patients with MPD.

4) People now sometimes use MPD as a **defence** for committing crimes, claiming they did not do the crimes and that another personality did. It would be easy to **fake** a case of MPD — little more than good acting skills would be required.

5) However, even if this trend in therapists once existed, and faking now occurs, these aren't reasons to dispute that the condition **does exist**.

## Case Studies Can Be *Unreliable*

There are a number of weaknesses of the Eve White case study:

1) The case study was reliant on **interviews**, so we have lots of 'rich' information that wouldn't be available through any other method.

**BUT**

2) Only one individual was studied, so it can't tell us anything about general trends in people — only about one person's individual **quirks**.

3) Case studies are more likely to be **retrospective**, relying on personal accounts from memory, which can be **biased**.

4) Case studies also suffer the possibility of **biased** information through the individual trying to **impress** the therapist, or saying what they think he/she **wants to hear**. However, in the case of Eve White, the therapists did try to corroborate their information by also interviewing relatives.

5) Case studies can also become **biased** because of the **therapist** or interviewer (often inadvertently) — they might only record what they want to hear, miss out important information, or skew the information to fit with their diagnosis or expectations.

Since watching *Many Limbed Dancing People*, everyone wanted to get in on the action.

Watch *The Three Faces of Eve* about Eve White, and watch *Sybil*... but don't watch *Me, Myself and Irene* — it's rubbish.

## Practice Questions

Q1 What are the clinical characteristics of MPD?

Q2 What does 'DID' stand for?

Q3 Who studied Eve White?

Q4 What was thought to have led to an increased diagnosis of MPD?

**Exam Questions**

Q1 Thigpen and Cleckley carried out a case study of multiple personality.
  a) Outline two limitations of this research method. [4 marks]
  b) Give one reason why a case study was used to collect data for this study. [2 marks]

## The best thing about me is there are so many of me...

*Thigpen and Cleckley don't really sound like psychologists. They sound like policemen in a children's book — Thigpen, Cleckley and Plod. PC Thigpen is tall and thin, and PC Cleckley is big and round. At the moment they're solving the big case of the missing sausages. I think the dog took them. There — wasn't that lovely, children? Now time for beddy-byes...*

# Summary of the Exam

*Last but not least, some useful information that'll help you score top marks in the exam. Worth a read I'd say...*

## There are **Two Exams**

1) You'll need to do **two exams** — **Psychological Investigations** which lasts for one hour, and **Core Studies** which is a two-hour exam.

2) In the **Psychological Investigations** paper, there'll be questions about pieces of research that have been carried out, and also a proposed piece of research. You'll need to use your knowledge of the various research techniques you've learnt about.

3) The paper contains **three sections of compulsory questions** and it's worth **60 marks**.

4) The **Core Studies** paper tests your knowledge of the 15 core studies and related issues that you'll have covered.

5) It contains three sections of questions. You must answer **all** of the questions in the **first** section. In the **second section** you are given **two** core studies to choose from and you have to answer **all** of the questions on your chosen study. In section 3 you'll need to **choose one** question to answer from a choice of two. In total, **120 marks** are available on this exam paper.

*Here's what you can expect to see in your **two AS Psychology** exams...*

## The Exam Papers Are **Broken Down** into Sections

The **Psychological Investigations** paper has **three** wonderful sections:

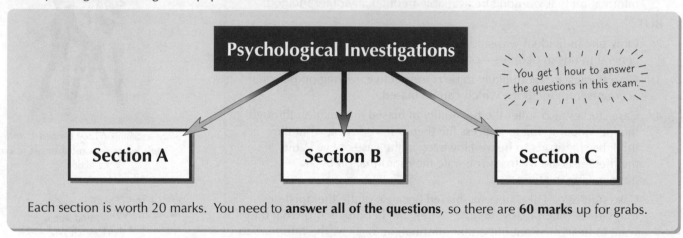

Each section is worth 20 marks. You need to **answer all of the questions**, so there are **60 marks** up for grabs.

The **Core Studies** paper has **three even more wonderful** sections:

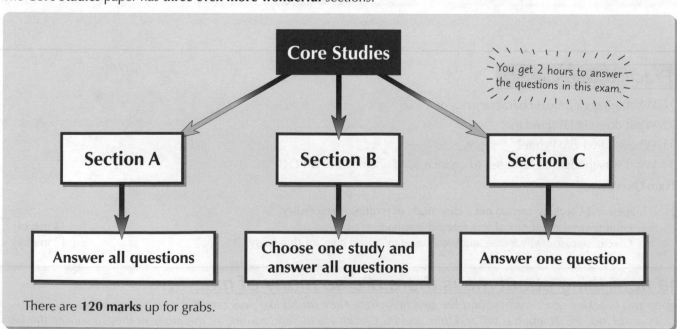

There are **120 marks** up for grabs.

# Assessment Objectives

*It really helps if you know what the examiner is looking for — luckily for you, this page can tell you...*

## You Need to Meet Certain Assessment Objectives

There are three assessment objectives covered by the unit exams — **AO1**, **AO2** and **AO3**.
The way that a question is **worded** can give away which assessment objective is being tested.

### AO1 is about the facts and theories

These questions cover the **knowledge and understanding of science**. You get marks by **recalling** and **describing** psychological knowledge, such as theories, studies and methods. For example, you might get asked to **describe a theory** of memory. To get the marks, you'd simply need to describe what the theory proposed and describe its key features. What you don't need to do is evaluate the theory — that'd just be a **waste of time** that you could use elsewhere, and you **won't get any extra marks**.

### AO2 gets you to apply your knowledge

AO2 questions are slightly different in that they get you to **apply your knowledge and understanding of science**. It's likely that these questions will begin with 'analyse' or 'evaluate'. Rather than just recalling stuff, e.g. listing relevant experiments, you've got to **apply your knowledge** to the situation in these questions. So, you'd need to use the experiments you've come up with to **support your argument**. You also might have to apply your knowledge to situations you've not come across before. For example, you could be asked to assess the **validity**, **reliability** or **credibility** of a study that's new to you.

### AO3 is about 'How Science Works'

'How Science Works' focuses on how scientific experiments are carried out. You need to be able to suggest appropriate **methodology** and know how to make sure measurements and observations are **accurate** and **precise**. You could also be asked to **analyse** and **evaluate** the **methodology** and **results** of a study described in the exam. When you're doing this, don't forget about things like **ethics** and **safety**.

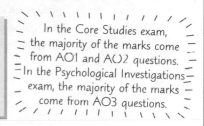

In the Core Studies exam, the majority of the marks come from AO1 and AO2 questions. In the Psychological Investigations exam, the majority of the marks come from AO3 questions.

## The Wording of the Question Can Tell You What to Do

1) For example, if the question simply asks you to '**describe**' or '**outline**' something, you know it's an **AO1** question. So you don't need to go into evaluating and explaining stuff.

2) Both **AO2** and **AO3** questions could ask you to **evaluate** something — but it's **what** you're asked to analyse that tells you which assessment objective is being covered:

- If the question asks you to evaluate a **theory**, it's an **AO2** question.
- If you're asked to evaluate the **method** or **results** of a study, you know it's an **AO3** question.

## The Number of Marks Tells You How Much to Write...

1) The number of marks that a question is worth gives you a pretty good clue of **how much to write**.
2) You get **one mark per correct point** made, so if a question is worth four marks, write four decent points.
3) There's no point writing a massive answer for a question that's only worth a few marks — it's a **waste of your time**.
4) For the longer essay-style questions, make sure that you've written **enough** to cover the 12 marks, but don't waffle.

## ...But You Can't Just Write About Anything

1) It's important to remember that it's not just a case of blindly scribbling down **everything** you can think of that's related to the subject. Doing this just **wastes time**, and it doesn't exactly impress the examiner.

2) You only get marks for stuff that's **relevant** and **answers the question**, so, make sure you read over the question a couple of times before you start writing so that you really understand what it's asking.

# Worked Questions

*The answers to the following set of questions would get you full marks in the exam...*

A psychologist used non-participant observation to investigate the relationship between the time spent playing violent video games and aggression levels in children. Her results are shown in the table below.

| Participant | Hours per week spent playing violent video games | Aggression rating |
|---|---|---|
| A | 5 | 7 |
| B | 4 | 5 |
| C | 2 | 4 |
| D | 8 | 6 |
| E | 9 | 10 |
| F | 1 | 2 |
| G | 7 | 8 |
| H | 6 | 5 |
| I | 10 | 9 |

1  (a)  Sketch a labelled scattergraph displaying the results of the study.  [4]

  (b)  Describe the relationship shown by the scattergraph you drew in part **(a)**.  [4]

2  Identify the independent variable and the dependent variable in this study.  [2]

3  (a)  The psychologist used opportunity sampling to obtain her sample.
    Outline **one** strength and **one** weakness of this sampling strategy.  [6]

  (b)  Outline **one** other type of sampling technique the researcher could have used.  [2]

4  What is meant by 'non-participant observation'?  [2]

**Total  [20]**

1 (a)

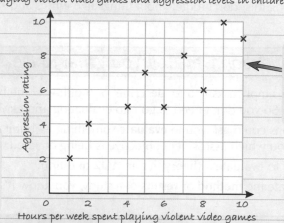

Scattergraph to show the relationship between time spent playing violent video games and aggression levels in children.

Make sure you plot your points carefully, and don't forget to label the axes and give your graph a title — it's an easy way to lose marks if you don't. There are 4 to pick up here.

Make sure you read the question carefully so that you know what you're being asked. For instance, this question just wants you to describe some findings — don't go into why you think the results are as they are.

1 (b)  As the amount of hours per week spent playing video games increases, so does aggression rating. This is a positive correlation.

This question asks for **one** strength and **one** weakness, so make sure that's all you give. Don't write more than one weakness — you won't get extra marks, so it's a waste of time.

2  The independent variable is the hours per week spent playing violent video games. The dependent variable is the aggression rating shown by the children.

3 (a)  Opportunity sampling is a quick and practical way of getting a sample. However, the sample is unlikely to be representative of a target group or population as a whole, which means the findings of the research can't be generalised.

3 (b)  The researcher could have used random sampling. This is where every member of the target group has an equal chance of being selected for the sample. This could be done by giving everyone in the target group a number and then getting a computer to randomly pick numbers to select the participants.

You could also have written about self-selected sampling here. Don't forget that if the question says 'outline' you just need to briefly describe it — you don't need to evaluate it.

4  Non-participant observation is a covert technique in which the researcher observes the activity without getting involved in it.

# Worked Questions

## An **Example** Core Studies (Section C) Essay That Would Get You **Full Marks**:

1  (a) Outline one assumption of the cognitive approach in psychology.  [2]
   (b) Describe how the cognitive approach could explain eyewitness testimony.  [4]
   (c) Describe one similarity and one difference between the Loftus and Palmer (1974) study and any other cognitive approach study.  [6]
   (d) Describe the strengths and limitations of the cognitive approach using examples from the Loftus and Palmer study.  [12]

(a) Cognitive psychology proposes that behaviour is the result of information processing involving perception, language, attention and memory.

> The question is only worth two marks, so keep it short and to the point.

(b) We make sense of information in a way that is meaningful to us. This means that we sometimes distort information, or fill in gaps, to help us make sense of something. This means that our memories can sometimes become distorted, leading to inaccuracies in eyewitness testimony.

(c) Another cognitive study was carried out by Loftus in 1979. One similarity between the studies is that they both investigated memory. Loftus and Palmer's study investigated participants' memory of a video of a car crash. Loftus' 1979 study investigated participants' memory of an individual depending on whether or not they were carrying a weapon.

> The other study doesn't need to be a core study — it can be any cognitive study you like.

However, in contrast to the Loftus and Palmer study, Loftus' 1979 study had high ecological validity as the participants weren't aware that the events they saw were staged. The Loftus and Palmer study was a laboratory experiment, and used an artificial video, reducing its ecological validity.

(d) Much of the research in the cognitive approach is carried out using laboratory experiments. This type of research has strengths and weaknesses. In laboratory experiments, the variables can be closely controlled, making the research very scientific and reliable. However, on the downside, laboratory experiments tend to lack ecological validity as they don't really reflect what we do in the real world. This makes it difficult to generalise the results to real-life situations.

> Don't waffle — make all information relevant to the question.

Loftus and Palmer's study is an example of this. The study was a laboratory experiment, meaning that the variables could be tightly controlled. This meant that the results were likely to be reliable. Another strength of this study is that the findings have been applied to real life — they led to the development of the cognitive interview technique, which has helped make eyewitness testimony more reliable. On the other hand, the laboratory setting made it difficult for the researchers to create a real-life situation — the stimulus in the study was a video of an artificial car crash. This may have meant that it was less emotionally arousing than it would be to see a car crash in real life. The experiment could have become one focusing on memory of watching television rather than eyewitness testimony. If this was the case, the results couldn't be generalised to other instances of eyewitness testimony.

> Relate your examples of strengths and weaknesses to points of the Loftus and Palmer study.

However, some cognitive psychology experiments do take place in a natural setting. Studies such as that by Loftus (1979) in which the participants weren't aware the events were staged, have more ecological validity as they tend to reflect real life. However, in this type of experiment there's usually less control of the variables.

> Problems can be general problems of all studies, not just specific ones.

> Sum up your answer with a brief conclusion — don't just repeat everything you've said in your answer.

In conclusion, the strengths and limitations of the cognitive approach depend on the type of research being carried out. Laboratory studies mean that the results are reliable but can lack ecological validity. In contrast, the results produced by field experiments can lack reliability but are usually ecologically valid.

## ... And Some **Final Pointers**...

1) You only get marks for stuff that's **relevant** and **answers the question**.

2) When you're writing your answer, try to **structure** it in an **organised** way. If there's one thing that examiners find worse than a load of pointless information, it's being unable to make head or tail of an answer.

3) Before you start, it might be worth jotting down a quick **plan** of what you want to write so that you don't end up with a really jumbled answer.

# Index

# Index

# Index